ALL
or Nothing

About the author

Mike McKinney is a registered clinical psychologist with over 20 years of experience. He has worked in both public (hospital-based) and private practice settings, and over the years has become increasingly intrigued by the potential for an individual's personality-style to enhance or undermine decisions and behaviours in relation to achievement. Mike is married to a psychologist and together they have two teenage boys. His interests include martial arts and classic Japanese motorcycles. Mike lives with his family in Christchurch, New Zealand.

ALL
or Nothing

Bringing balance to the
achievement-oriented
personality

MIKE McKINNEY

First published 2016

Exisle Publishing Pty Ltd
'Moonrising', Narone Creek Road, Wollombi, NSW 2325, Australia
P.O. Box 60–490, Titirangi, Auckland 0642, New Zealand
www.exislepublishing.com

A CiP record for this book is available from the National Library of Australia.

ISBN 978-1-925335-26-2

Designed by Nick Turzynski, redinc. Book Design
Typeset in Source Sans Pro 11.5/18
Printed in China

This book uses paper sourced under ISO 14001 guidelines from well-managed forests and other controlled sources.

10 9 8 7 6 5 4 3 2 1

Disclaimer
This book is a general guide only and should never be a substitute for the skill, knowledge and experience of a qualified medical professional dealing with the facts, circumstances and symptoms of a particular case. The information presented in this book is based on the research, training and professional experience of the author, and is true and complete to the best of their knowledge. However, this book is intended only as an informative guide; it is not intended to replace or countermand the advice given by the reader's personal physician or healthcare professional. Because each person and situation is unique, the author and the publisher urge the reader to check with a qualified healthcare professional before using any procedure where there is a question as to its appropriateness. The author, publisher and their distributors are not responsible for any adverse effects or consequences resulting from the use of the information in this book. It is the responsibility of the reader to consult a physician or other qualified healthcare professional regarding their personal care. This book contains references to products that may not be available everywhere. The intent of the information provided is to be helpful; however, there is no guarantee of results associated with the information provided.

To one of the best psychologists I have ever worked with and who also happens to be my wife. Thanks for all the unquestioning support with this project. Also, much appreciation and admiration to my two teenage sons for their discussions around the dinner table. Your understanding of human nature is way beyond your years.

Contents

Introduction

There are many arenas where dedication and focus are central to distinguishing oneself, of which the corporate world, competitive sport and the performing arts are prime examples.

Undoubtedly a degree of single-mindedness comes in handy in these and other environments, and will help you become competitive and therefore, hopefully, successful. But what if that same drive and determination excludes so much more of life? What if you have to sacrifice your relationships or your wellbeing in pursuit of your career goals?

All or Nothing is for people who are goal-directed (some may say in the extreme) and use all their focus and energy to complete tasks, despite any unintended personal costs and consequences.

However, this book does not assume that trying hard and having goals is wrong. There is no doubt that pushing oneself is a prerequisite for attaining high levels in the competitive business world. This is readily acknowledged by the author and there is no vested interest here to promote the 'everyone's a winner' thesis. Nor am I trying to suggest that people should not chase their dreams or continue to aim high. *All or Nothing* will help you make positive choices — choices based on information and understanding rather than habitual responses. It is about (and for) individuals who have a strong drive to achieve and regularly push themselves, perhaps beyond their tolerance levels. It is this determination that is at once the greatest strength of such people, yet also potentially their greatest vulnerability.

This book provides real-world understanding of the 'all or nothing', or A/N, personality-style that can be encountered in all areas of life. This approach to life is an expression of a series of personality characteristics common to many high achievers but also people who push themselves to meet their goals in a wide range of domains and careers. This way of interacting with the world usually encompasses a high degree of determination, persistence and focus on goals. Additionally, this can be to the exclusion of everything else, which is a key aspect of the 'all or nothing' way of life. Such an approach to life can be positive and can reinforce the idea that the more you put into a task, the sooner you get the rewards from your efforts. However, a little like a hamster on its wheel, once onto this way of behaving, an A/N individual can find it hard to stop.

The A/N personality-style is particularly prevalent within the business world.

CASE STUDY

Matthew (not his real name) was the CEO of a large institution. For many years he had provided direction, support and leadership to the organization as a whole and also to the staff who worked for him. He approached the role with an attention to detail that was second to none and he prioritized the needs of the organization above all else. However, alongside this was a strong perfectionistic drive. This meant that things did not get signed off or leave the building until they were first rate and entirely completed! Matthew came to me as he had experienced some significant challenges with his mood, to the point that he ended up resigning from his position. This man of intellect and significant experience was at a loss to understand (let alone explain) how he had come to this point — was he not the one who fixed things for others and successfully juggled a multitude of issues and events?

It wasn't until we began exploring some of the build-up to this situation, along with the day-to-day pressures of his role, that Matthew came to see that he had experienced what the business world might call burn-out. This very capable, thoughtful and driven individual had forgotten to take care of himself while putting out corporate fires left, right and centre. It soon became clear that a lot had been sacrificed outside the work environment. In essence, and without realizing it, this dedicated man had become so focused on his role that he had pushed himself physically and mentally beyond his limits. Matthew's internal drivers, dedication to the job and readiness to meet all challenges had taken a toll that was both professional and personal. He had paid a high price but also came to realize that, with a little help, all was not lost and that he could reconfigure his sense of self, rebuild aspects of important relationships plus explore ways to return to employment — in a manner that was perhaps more sustainable. After Matthew left his role, a review was conducted to ensure that the high levels of performance could be maintained within the organization; he was subsequently replaced with 2.5 people!

The drive to produce this book came from my practice as a clinical psychologist. One of the things psychologists are taught is to look for patterns, reflect upon how they might have come about and then identify whether they are helpful to the individual or not. In my career of over twenty years, I have worked with people from a wide range of backgrounds and I have seen many behaviours — some helpful and some downright destructive. I have been struck, though, by clients who (as either their presenting problem or one attached to their presenting problem) have demonstrated a remarkably consistent pattern of A/N behaviours. These behaviours have, on the one hand, helped the person achieve in their chosen direction in life but also may have (paradoxically) restricted or even prevented them from achieving to their full potential. Often, it was not until 'too late' that the person realized such a focused approach may have cost them the very thing/s they were striving towards: their career, appropriate recognition and, sometimes, their family life.

NOT A DIFFERENT SPECIES

People exhibiting A/N personality traits come from both genders and are of all ages, backgrounds and roles in life. Although A/N individuals often get labelled as such by peers and family members, it is important to realize they do not have obsessive compulsive disorder (OCD). This is a psychiatric diagnosis, and it seems to be the strong drive to complete tasks/goals that leads other people to label A/N individuals as obsessive. Rather than this essentially medical definition, I prefer to use the term 'personality-style', which captures the fact the A/N behaviours are an integral part of the person and are expressed within their usual world events. I do not suggest A/N people are riddled with pathological behaviours, nor are they held captive by a dysfunctional personality. However, such people are indeed driven and this can take them to a place where they sometimes lose perspective and balance in their pursuit of attainment, completion and perfection.

A/N people are not just at the higher levels of business, sport and artistic fields. They can also be weekend warriors who tirelessly strive and become totally immersed in their training for events such as triathlons and marathons. The common theme is passion, underscored by a strong focus and desire to excel or transcend. However, this can also mean a single-mindedness regarding the goal, which can result in other (previously important) tasks and roles struggling to find time within the busy schedule.

The book will outline how an A/N personality-style and approach presents itself and the problems that can potentially result — case studies will be used to shed further light on how aspects of this personality-style affect a person's life. This will help you identify if, and to what extent, you experience, live with and exhibit the relevant traits. While the book will present some theoretical approaches from the world of psychology, these are presented in a manner that allows them to be easily digested and, more importantly, related to. Of course, just describing an issue is of little value in itself; on its own, awareness is simply a recipe for frustration. Therefore, throughout the book, suggestions on things to be aware of will be complemented by actions you can take to bring about some level of change.

A key aim is to help you understand the costs of certain behaviours, understand what you are doing, how (and possibly why) this came about and then take yourself to the point where you feel empowered to do something about it . . . if you choose. The book does not advocate the 'stopping' of all behaviours associated with an A/N approach to life; to do this would simply be to follow the root issue associated with this condition — either 'I do it all' or 'I stop it all'. There is much that is positive within the approach of being focused, hard-working and keen to excel. The difficulty comes when one direction is pursued to the exclusion of all others. Learning to 'dial in and dial out' your levels of effort, as appropriate to the situational demands, will potentially bring about more sustainable engagement that helps maximize quality of life *and* potential. Think of a dimmer attached to a light switch. Previously, incandescent light was brought about by turning a switch on and then ended by turning the switch off. There was power coming to the bulb or there wasn't; there was light in the room or there wasn't. However, a dimmer can now be attached to the switch. This gives you the ability to use the power in a manner that provides light in proportion to your needs at a given time. So if you want to read a novel in the evening, you might turn the dimmer switch up for more light. Conversely, if you want to chill out with a nice glass of sauvignon blanc while listening to some soothing jazz, you have the choice of lowering the light level via the dimmer. Neither of these lighting levels is 'correct', nor is one 'wrong'. Rather, by having a mechanism to adjust the light, a more suitable atmosphere can be obtained for the desired activity. Perhaps the same can be achieved with our level of engagement on tasks within our work environment and life in general?

WHY SHOULD YOU READ THIS BOOK?

I hope that by the time you get to the end of this book, you will see that you can still achieve and extend yourself without sacrificing your personal and family life or previously enjoyed activities. Being successful does not need to undermine your physical or mental health and wellbeing. But if it is costing this, then after reading this book you will hopefully be in a better, more informed position to make choices that are right for you while ensuring that your behaviours are in alignment with your values and goals. It would be great if I can help you become more flexible in your approach to your career and life in general.

Your ability to maintain this change in approach will be supported by a range of tools and approaches explained throughout the book, based on psychological theory, practice and principles. *There is no need to completely change who you are.* Rather, it is about learning to reconfigure your sense of self, beginning to tolerate uncertainty and potentially developing a more meaningful and multi-faceted life — while still achieving. If you have become tired from pushing yourself relentlessly, if you are sick of psychologically beating yourself up, if you have come to see that a large paycheque is not as fulfilling as once hoped (how many Lamborghinis can you fit in a garage anyway?), this book may just be for you. It may even offer you a life-changing opportunity. Feel free to be sceptical but do try to be open and honest with yourself. No one is going to judge you if you say to yourself, 'Yep, that's me all right.' That is the beauty of reading a book: it happens inside your head, it is a private and personal moment that can offer the chance for reflection based on a new insight or perspective.

So, take a risk and read on.

1 How do I know if I am 'all or nothing'?

This chapter provides an outline of some key aspects and attributes of a less-than-balanced approach to life. You might identify with some or most of the descriptions as you read this chapter. Either will be correct, as this is not about providing a 'diagnosis' of A/N behaviour. Rather, it is about helping you become more aware of personal characteristics that help you to achieve but, at other times, work against you.

Undoubtedly there are many people in the business world who demonstrate the A/N personality-style. An example is Bernie Ecclestone, the mastermind behind Formula 1 motor racing. This focused businessman runs an incredibly successful, worldwide empire. This 84-year-old reportedly has an insatiable appetite for work, an energy level that seems other-worldly and a perfectionistic streak that is both powerful and directed. He seems to live, breathe and 'do' his business all day and every day — but does this come at the exclusion of other aspects of his life? In 2013 he conducted an interview (subsequently published in *The Times*) in his chauffeur-driven car on the way to a family christening. During the interview, Mr Ecclestone told the reporter: 'If I didn't get up in the morning knowing I have a few problems to solve, I wouldn't get up.' On another occasion, he replied to a question on the quality of his life and what made him happy by saying, 'I'm not sure what happiness is. I have experienced satisfaction when I have planned something and it has come off.' Mr Ecclestone has had some challenges in his relationships over time and acknowledged that his most recent wife left him because '… I can't take time off'. This is a man who essentially created the hugely successful spectacle that Formula 1 is today. He is reportedly worth vast sums of money and controls all aspects of the empire basically by himself. He is by any measure a hugely successful individual — who (surprise, surprise) returned to work almost immediately after having a triple coronary bypass. From an external perspective, it would seem that he embodies and lives the A/N approach to life that this book is about.

IS IT ME, THOUGH?

An A/N individual has many positive attributes, not the least of which is the ability to focus on a task and see it through to completion. This has many reinforcing aspects in that such people are praised for their achievements and also are self-reinforced for their efforts. The A/N individual tends to prioritize the immediate, positive outcomes such as completion, which then become both a motivator and a reinforcer. To this end, the person is willing to trade off other, potentially competing demands and activities in order to meet the self-generated goal. Being busy is a central theme of an A/N person's life and this busyness is always in service of a particular goal e.g. short-term projects or longer-term career strategies. Although the person might be given tasks to do by an employer or manager, an important element is their internal drive. This is a motivational force that will help block out distractions and competing demands. Such an ability to filter out distractions and 'unnecessary' events allows the focus to be complete and sets the scene for undisturbed application of effort.

In this case, there appears to be but one way to move forward and that invariably involves pushing oneself. While this is useful for achieving and completing, it can come at a cost. The individual can overlook outcomes that are not necessarily obvious but may be building up. Such costs can be health related, socially oriented, familial or recreational. This totality of focus often means these 'other' issues or tasks are downgraded in importance — not purposely, it must be said, but because they don't fit the current brief and therefore are simply not registered. Over time, this approach can become a self-perpetuating system that limits and narrows awareness, which further reduces the potential for flexibility. Thus, the concept of balance in life can be lost, or at least not thought about. Time away from the current goal or activity is seen as a problem and life can eventually hit a tipping point whereby other interests, obligations and relationships start to take a back seat. Once fully engaged in a task, strong aspects of the personality (such as a sense of responsibility and commitment) start to kick in and this makes it increasingly hard to shift from the main focus. Part of why this is difficult is that task completion can be intimately intertwined with the need to do a perfect job. Ceasing a task partway through seems to equate with a sense of failure and this fear of failure can be the driver of much of the behaviour that has become 'all or nothing'.

Once commenced, a goal or commitment can come to dominate the thinking, perspective and options identified by an A/N individual. This is where the difficulties with being flexible come in. The A/N person finds it hard to hold in their head that balance might be possible, whereby more than one option can be held, nurtured and worked towards at the same time. What tends to stand out is the competing nature of two or more activities and the potential that this will mean less time for the key project and, therefore, quality will surely suffer. Struggling with flexibility, the person locks themself down to the main job and shuts out other distractions. The result is a dedicated, focused and full-on effort to complete the goal, whether it be immediate, short-term or long-term. The perfectionistic part of the personality then starts to kick in, which raises the threat of poor performance and potential embarrassment associated with that dreaded word: *failure*. It is important to understand these threats are not necessarily clearly understood or identified as such by the person; indeed, they might be experienced more as a 'feeling'. This can be something that is hard for the person to describe, yet it brings about a sense of unease. The person is therefore motivated to avoid this discomfort and the perceived negative consequences e.g. non-completion of the goal. This results in further effort and an even greater narrowing of focus, which essentially shuts out the rest of the world. However, this can become a trap. The drive to stave off the feelings of failure becomes stronger and the A/N person will do just about anything to avoid either poor performance or judgment by others. This inevitably results in more effort and/or longer hours focused on the job at hand.

There is often a strong inner critic which is hard to escape as the voice is part of the self, is confident with its comments and tends to operate on a no-holds-barred approach to passing judgment on how you are performing. The aim is to show where the problem is, who the author of this disaster is — you — and to bully you into doing more, therefore hopefully meeting the goals originally set or agreed to. It doesn't matter that these goals may have been unrealistic in terms of timeframes or extent. A part of the fear for an A/N individual is that they will be judged by significant others (e.g. their boss, coach or mentor) and be deemed to be operating poorly or not up to the required standard. One of the outcomes of this concern is a reduction in the ability to fairly and realistically monitor their own performance. As a result, A/N people can question their true ability and can also start to consider that they are not up to standard.

Jason is a senior-level financial executive responsible for several departments and decisions relating to large sums of money. He has been successfully employed by his company for a number of years and rose to this senior position due to his performance and ability. However, behind this public persona is a man who experiences self-doubt regarding his skill-set and ability to sustain performance levels. When he sought some therapeutic input, Jason described to me classic symptoms of burn-out such as loss of interest in the role, reduced sense of engagement with the company and colleagues plus struggling to energize himself as he previously had.

It soon became clear that Jason was a hard-working perfectionist with a powerful drive to complete his tasks on time and to a very high standard. He prioritized the work, plus the many responsibilities that accompanied this, above all other aspects of his life. However, Jason was becoming increasingly anxious that he would not be able to live up to his own expectations or those of others at work. His response to this was to work harder and longer, but this only drained his personal resources further and the anxiety continued to increase — as did his self-doubt — in a vicious cycle. He became overwhelmed and his worst fear (not performing) was becoming a reality.

Jason ended up taking extended sick leave due to the high anxiety and a lowering mood.

SOUNDS FAMILIAR, BUT IS IT REALLY AN ISSUE?

Unfortunately, this sometimes fragile sense of self can be challenged further by the situation that A/N people such as Jason find themselves in. The trap tightens more at this point because the internal clash starts to present itself more clearly. How do you relate to this talented and achieving image of yourself while being concerned that it might all be an illusion, one that is about to be torn apart at any time by the discovery of your incompetence? This is an important point, as it signals a shift from feeling in control to entering a zone characterized by self-doubt and a sense of being judged harshly. Unfortunately, emotions are powerful but somewhat irrational masters. The problem is that potential 'failure' strikes at the personal identity and you are faced with a sense of being unable to meet your usual high standards.

Unfortunately, at such times the internal critic can step up a gear and become more insistent. This can see the A/N person rely on the time-tested and automatic approach of pushing themselves even harder. If this well-rehearsed behaviour fails to bring about a different result (e.g. the task is not completed as expected) confidence can start to decrease. Because you have been so busy focusing on the goal or project, you can drift away from friends and not engage in general life activities as in the past. By throwing yourself into work so fully (with no consideration of balance in your life) there can be little to bolster you in challenging times. As an A/N individual, you may also become vulnerable to internal messages around poor performance.

Even though they often appear confident, A/N people can be acutely aware of, and vulnerable to, the expectations of others, such as those important to the project or task at hand, for example employers, departmental leaders or colleagues. An A/N person can therefore be prone to second guessing the intentions, beliefs and interpretations of people who have influence on their career. Such a situation can result in over-identification with responses from others and therefore perceptions of being judged. As already discussed, effort (cognitive and/or physical) might therefore be increased to try to deliver what is believed to be necessary. However, if the perception is incorrect, then much effort can be wasted and precious resources potentially further diminished.

Attempting to second-guess is not always helpful. The A/N person has lots of motivation to achieve but does not account for their own welfare (this doesn't register on a radar which is attuned to the external expectations) so once again, family, friends, health and hobbies may be shunted to the rear. Part of what happens at this point is an engagement of the dichotomous thinking process that many A/N people use to help make sense of their world. This thinking identifies things as relevant or irrelevant, goal directed or frivolous, useful or a waste of space. Such a style of thinking keeps the person focused on the goal at hand and allows a speedy appraisal of 'not-so-important' activities as possibly being counterproductive.

A POWERFUL COMBINATION

The combination of high expectations and motivation is a powerful one and can see you persisting with tasks when others might have called a halt. This can be positive with regard to deadlines or the meeting of a performance goal. However, it can be unhelpful when self-monitoring is suspended in deference to the bigger goal. The only variables accounted for at such times are those directly related to the outcome of the project at hand. Perhaps not such an issue if the project is measured in hours or days but potentially problematic if it relates to an ongoing role or longer-term goal such as a career pathway.

An interesting twist is the challenge for some A/N people in saying no to requests related to the topic they are engaged in. They can find it hard to turn away requests for assistance or to take on extra work related to the current project. This is especially so if it comes from a perceived superior or colleagues also involved in the focal task. Why is this so hard? As the A/N person can be sensitive to potential criticism, they are therefore usually keen to avoid changes to their ranking. Although in reality there might not be a huge threat, the potential of such can be enough to make the person agree to the request even if they don't have enough time to help out. Within the person a battle begins regarding possible failure (i.e. failure to be the same as others of a similar standing or to measure up to their own standards). The latter probably exerts the greatest influence over the difficulty to say no as there is a 'Harsh Internal Critic' lurking inside most A/N individuals who is ever ready to point out failings, either current or potential. Unfortunately, this can drive the person harder so as to avoid this self-denigration. It is important to realize that it is not just the words or harsh tone that are unsettling. Rather, it is the potential of being faced with the image of not being who you feel you should be that is so worrying.

CASE STUDY

Tessa had established herself as a professional ballet dancer with several international companies. However, this high-achieving woman was now attempting to come to terms with the long-term physical problems she had developed as a result of her intense physical lifestyle.

Tessa described being raised in a family that valued the arts, and her parents thought ballet would be an excellent 'career choice' for their daughter, even though she was only around five when she started dancing. Tessa apparently showed a natural aptitude for ballet and this was enhanced by the extra classes her parents paid for. This led to success in competitions and then scholarships and, ultimately, a place in a professional company.

Tessa's parents were both perfectionists and expected high levels of commitment and success from their daughter from an early age. She recalls feeling much pressure to meet these standards but also noted that she was (increasingly) demanding much of herself. As the years went by, Tessa struggled with eating challenges (in order to maintain weight goals) plus a variety of injuries brought about from the gruelling training regimes that she endured. Tessa readily acknowledged that she supplemented the group training with her own after-hours practice, which impacted her ability to take time out and relax. Eventually, Tessa developed stress fractures in her lower leg. She was strongly encouraged by medical advisors to take time off to heal. However, this was unthinkable to a young woman who was dancing in a very competitive environment, who had extremely high expectations of herself and was following her passion.

Unfortunately, this passion and drive eventually cost Tessa the thing she loved the most — her dancing career — as the stress fractures went on to become full fractures of the lower leg.

THE COST OF THIS BEHAVIOUR

All-or-nothing behaviour affects people in all areas of society, not just high-achieving professionals. There are legions of amateur athletes around the globe who exhibit high levels of dedication and focus for their passion. Similarly, many people in their everyday family or social lives exhibit an intense level of focus and participation. For many of these people, so much can be invested in one issue/approach that their sense of self and personal worth becomes wrapped up in this way of viewing and responding to the world. They also have limited time to nurture aspects of themselves that previously were important. As a result, their interests, focus and efforts become channelled into a narrower stream of life and there can be a loss of balance.

One of the key aspects of the A/N personality-style is an automatic response to long-standing or core beliefs (often referred to as schemas) plus using well-rehearsed behaviours in an automatic manner. Difficulty with shifting to alternative perspectives or another way of approaching a task is often experienced. In this case a person can, for example, be so focused on getting into the office that they step into the same pothole on a daily basis then, instead of changing their walking route, repeatedly curse the local council for not doing their job properly. This dogged (or is that stubborn?) determination to get to the end of the task can result in the person repeatedly pushing beyond their physical and emotional tolerance level. However, if this is not sustainable or the goal is not achievable, they may feel compelled to walk away, an outcome seen as impossible to avoid by some A/N people — for surely, there is no point in continuing if the goal cannot be reached and the task cannot be done in the manner expected?

At this point, certain aspects of life can come to a grinding halt and the costs of the overly focused, goal-directed behaviour can come rushing in. These costs may have been quietly building up over time, a bit like a psychological mortgage that hasn't been paid and the bank is now calling in the loan, with interest. For many such people, it is the decline in their physical health or the appearance of anxiety or depression that forces them to finally hop off this real-life merry-go-round of pushing themselves to achieve at ever increasing standards. This can hit with a thump, as the person tends not to have considered the delayed negative results, their focus lying elsewhere.

There can be a tipping point where the benefits (real or hoped for) are outweighed by the personal costs. Even if the challenges become obvious to the individual and they want to change, it is never quite that simple. It is not enough for the A/N person to just realize something is 'wrong' or to be made aware of risk factors to look out for; such individuals need to understand what's behind the behaviours they engage in and the personal drivers that so regularly come into play. They can benefit from hearing that change is possible but also by seeing that all will not be lost if they do try to change — for the fear is often that if s/he changes, they must change completely.

IN SUMMARY

'All or nothing' is an approach to and way of engaging with life. It is an expression of personal characteristics. It is also something that has helped you achieve, potentially to high levels. It is not a personality disorder, nor is it a psychiatric condition. However, it can result in a dichotomous way of viewing the world. This means you see things as perfect or useless, beautiful or ugly, a pass or a fail.

There is not a specific number of symptoms that identify a person as A/N, nor does it require a professional 'diagnosis' as such. There are, however, a number of descriptors and behaviours that give some indication as to whether you might operate in this manner. Take a moment to review the descriptors below and see if there is a degree of fit for you with this approach to life.

Try this

Take a moment to reflect on the following questions.

Do you:

- tend to approach life with singular purpose
- expect highly of yourself
- have a strongly developed sense of responsibility
- focus on a single goal to the exclusion of all else
- push yourself to achieve, despite costs to yourself
- chastise yourself in a harsh and repeated manner
- find that the need for perfection is strong and dictates how you behave
- see compromise as a swear-word and something you can't relate to
- describe yourself as goal-directed or as a 'driven' personality
- feel somewhat inadequate or a bit of a fraud, despite doing well in your chosen field?

Have you found:

- your life is out of balance
- it is difficult to have a broad perspective on issues
- one issue or role tends to dominate your life
- connections to family and friends have slipped away at times

- completion of certain tasks comes above all else
- your confidence can be variable and fear of failure is strong
- it is hard to be flexible and see other options
- timeframes and expectations you set for yourself may be unrealistic
- it is difficult to say no to others, especially to 'important' people
- you respond and behave in routine ways to familiar situations?

ASPECTS FOR REFLECTION, OPTIONS FOR CHANGE

There is no need to make sudden changes and become a brand new person. At this stage you simply need to reflect on the information you have just read. Indeed, it is like going shopping for new clothes, where you now take time to consider the size and fit — is this immediately comfortable or will it take a while to get used to? Action does not need to come immediately; however, reading and reflecting can help things make more sense.

If you can relate to the information and descriptions in this chapter, then read on and be open to what may be ahead. While doing this, pause and review your life experiences to see if they fit with what you have just read. Please try to resist the tendency to judge whatever aspects or behaviours you are reflecting upon. Rather, just ask if the ways you have responded within the important domains of your life might be consistent with what you have read. If so, consider investing some more of your time in learning about the A/N personality-style and what this might mean in the longer term for you as an individual, a professional, a partner or a family member.

Remember that there isn't, nor does there have to be, a perfect fit or example of *anything*. You might, for example, only relate to some aspects. This is fine, for as we shall see, things do not need to be either/or. However, it can still be beneficial to understand how these aspects of your life have come in to play and what maintains them over such a long period of time.

· · · · · · · · · · · · · · · · · · · ·

Read on, but continue to take some time each day to reflect upon what you are reading and see if there is any merit in considering options to adjust or alter. This is *not* about creating a new you or completely changing your personality. Rather, it is about reconfiguring your sense of self and allowing aspects of yourself to return to the fore after having been overrun by well-rehearsed ways of interacting with the world.

2 Where (and why) did this begin?

Most A/N types have been behaving the same way for a long time — the executive who works all hours and the triathlete who trains every day did not just suddenly become like that. But these behaviours, often exhibited across a range of areas (or domains) of life, can become more obvious (and also potentially problematic) once the person finds their niche in life. No matter which environment the behaviour is expressed in, A/N individuals share some key attributes. Prime amongst these is an orientation towards perfection, a drive to succeed and a readiness to push themselves to meet their goal/s. The question is whether these attributes were made, developed or stumbled upon.

WHERE WE COME FROM CAN BE IMPORTANT

If you ask A/N people what their earliest recollections of such behaviours are, they often state that their family of origin had a set of values that revolved around meeting goals and/or having high standards. Allied with this may have been expectations around performance and involvement in tasks e.g. homework and chores being completed to a high standard. The person's parents might have been people who worked hard, prioritized completion and valued good outcomes. Thus, there was potentially a good degree of modelling involved. This would have been observed, if not yet fully understood, by the child. By watching a credible role model — someone important, trusted, respected (or feared) — engage in tasks and repeatedly respond in a particular way, the child starts to accept that this is how things are done.

Within the family, contingencies will operate that reinforce certain behaviours and approaches, such as completing a task *before* moving on to more enjoyable activities. These expectations might be referred to regularly, so that they become part of how the family operates. Positive reinforcement may also flow more readily when the child meets the expectations so s/he learns that working hard, fast and to a good standard are valued by significant others. Additionally, these ways of behaving lead to social reinforcement, positive standing and possibly rewards (e.g. treats or pocket money). Conversely, not performing to a certain level or in a manner consistent with expectations may lead to a cost, such as punishment or loss of access to rewards. Such learning is powerful. If the standards are set and reinforced by significant others, a strong desire to please others by meeting these expectations can develop.

Over time, such expectations can become part of the family ethos, culture and experience. The norms are set and determine behaviour for those in the family system. The young person will then take these beliefs and expectations of behaviour with them as they move outside of the family environment and into other circles, such as school or sporting arenas. Even at a relatively early age, children can demonstrate a focus on task completion and quality of engagement. If this is connected with positive outcomes (e.g. a sense of success or acknowledgment) the child will be more likely to repeat the behaviour/s.

Competition

If the child is competitive, the sporting arena, which has a focus on competing and winning, may well appeal and bring out or enhance that aspect of behaviour. It is important to acknowledge that some individuals are naturally competitive and will seek out competition and try their hardest with each event they participate in. It is also true that children can build on their natural competitiveness if they have parents who value such attributes. Feedback from a competitive and driven parent may reinforce the need to train hard and play harder with an emphasis on winning — 'There are no prizes for coming second', 'You don't win the silver; you lose the gold'. Consistent messages such as these, from important or influential people, will promote certain behaviours and ways of approaching games. If similar behaviours are expressed in different settings (i.e. at home and on the sports field), a process of generalization has begun. This is where environments that seem similar bring about expressions of similar behaviours because these behaviours (e.g. pushing oneself) worked in the original setting. As a result, the person will respond to these and, thereafter, similar settings by doing things in the same way; the behaviour can then become firmly entrenched and eventually automatic.

The single-minded focus can also be fostered from an early age by choosing similar behaving peers and engaging with groups where such an approach is valued. This reinforces particular behaviours and perspectives and it does this in a selective manner: one whereby similar ways of thinking and behaving are reinforced while diverging approaches are ignored. This effectively selects out certain behaviours, thus maintaining a particular culture of the group. There is often low tolerance within competitive peer groups for individuals not demonstrating effort or achieving at expected levels. Few people, especially at a young age, want to be different so the drive to perform and meet expectations is set up and maintained by social pressures. Fear of ostracism is strong in young people (especially teens) and can therefore make adherence to behavioural expectations a strong driving force. This can see key behaviours such as pushing oneself, prioritizing goals and having high expectations become a 'usual' part of the person's approach to life.

Control

Somewhat different to the competitive parent is the parent whose approach and expectations relate to maintaining control. These people often place emphasis on high and potentially unrealistic expectations. However, such expectations are not necessarily in the service of enhancing the child. Rather, the emphasis is on a power differential with a parenting style that can be based around orderliness and obedience. The controlling nature of such parents leaves little room for variability in meeting targets. The consequences of poor performance can be swift, and this can teach a lesson about the place and value of one's own needs plus the importance of prioritizing the expected outcome.

One of the most problematic behaviours within this family system is that affirmation can be contingent — that is, it depends on some condition being met, usually upon performance at or above a certain level. Once the standard is met, affection and attention tend to be offered. Conversely, if the level is not achieved, affection may be withheld or removed. Of potential relevance to the developing child is that affirmation might not be given for anything less than meeting the expected standard. The young person can therefore struggle to develop flexibility in how they respond to events in life. The child unfortunately learns that 'good enough' does not exist or that it is something to avoid at all costs.

Another challenge with such parents is that they may not confine their comments and responses to the child's performance. Unfortunately, they may also personalize it in a negative or undermining manner. Thus, the feedback might not be about the task being difficult but more that the child is at fault or that s/he is unable to produce the goods as expected. As a result, a demanding cycle can be set up whereby the child learns that to be valued (by those most important to him/her) they must go about their tasks in a single-minded fashion. If a parent behaves coldly to the child (who has by now picked up that the parent values high effort and perfect outcomes) then the child can end up pushing themselves to both please and achieve. But note that the desire for a positive outcome is related to an external party. There is no intrinsic motivation or self-generated ideal here. Rather, a child (desiring affection and/or attention) is learning to perform in a manner that maximizes the chances they will be acknowledged and given some affection.

The delivery of rewards is now contingent upon a positive or particular outcome being reached. Over time, this can shift the perspective ever more firmly in an external direction, whereby one's own needs, tiredness and limits are ignored in pursuit of the achievement. Although this behaviour was originally related directly to obtaining affection, it will gradually morph over time to focusing on the goal completion or perfect performance itself. The original aspect of seeking reinforcement has now become wrapped up in ways of behaving to achieve certain goals. Although the parent may no longer be the main driver of such behaviour, parental substitutes — teachers, coaches or employers — can assume the same role, which intermittently reinforces the dedicated focus, high level of performance and non-questioning approach to activity. Finally, the (eventual) major driver of such behaviour becomes the individual themselves. This can see the person internalize the standards and expectations so that they become their own worst critic and drive themselves to achieve at very high standards.

. . . .

An amazing first-person account of the A/N personality-style and the effects of early upbringing can be found in the autobiography of former world number one tennis player, Andre Agassi. This honest, insightful but raw account of Agassi's rise to fame provides a personal narrative of many of the factors contained in this book. Agassi details a struggle with standards which were too high and, indeed, unsustainable. These were not developed by him nor were they encountered by chance. Rather, they were proscribed, enforced and reinforced by his father. This myopic parent apparently had a goal to have a child who would not only become a professional tennis player but also number one in the world. In among the various challenges, achievements and relationships in the book is a thread which weaves a story of someone who was set up to perform and then shown how to push himself beyond personal limits. It is a first-hand account of what the life of a top-level sportsperson (who operated consistently in an A/N manner) was like from the beginning. This is not to suggest that Agassi is a 'prototypical' example of A/N behaviour, nor that every other A/N person operates in the same way. It is however, interesting to read the real-life battles he had with self-criticism (and, at times, self-loathing) and perfectionism. Agassi also describes in vivid terms what this struggle with perfectionism was like: '… perfection isn't the goal in our house, it's the law. If you're not perfect, you're a loser.' Perfectionism is often a central feature of the A/N person's life and drive; it will be explored more fully in Chapter 6.

Agassi describes a torturous journey through life, whereby he takes on (reluctantly, yet powerfully) the approach to judgment modelled by his father. At one point he outlines the transition from being the receiver of harsh criticism to becoming a finely tuned purveyor of the same: 'I've internalised my father — his impatience, his perfectionism, his rage — until his voice doesn't just feel like my own, it is my own, I no longer need my father to torture me. From this day on, I can do it all by myself.' This gives us an example of the harsh inner critic that can play a critical role in keeping expectations around high levels of performance firmly in the forefront of the A/N individual's world.

BEING UNSURE CAN SHAPE OUR BEHAVIOUR

The developing A/N personality comes to realize there is much riding on the outcome of any venture. This can impact behaviour but also on personal confidence levels and decision making before even beginning something. It can become scary to actually start a task for, once begun, the performance is open to scrutiny by parents, teachers, coaches and the like.

Unfortunately, the A/N youngster starts to live and behave within a closed system whereby there appears to be only two possible outcomes from behaviour: success or failure. While this might not be the reality, the developing A/N personality tends to operate in this manner and therefore can conceive of only these two results. One of these, of course, is more acceptable to the self than the other.

Over time, fear of failure can become associated with the drive to succeed. This developing fear can have an effect on the type and level of behaviours put in place and the young person may even begin to hold back from starting tasks at all. They might put it off for a long time, often until there is no choice (via pressure from parents, for example, or a school deadline looming) but to get underway. Interestingly, this lack of commencement can be seen by others as tardiness or being 'too laid back'. The issue is perhaps better identified as procrastination but this might not be due to laziness or lack of motivation. Rather, the A/N youngster is faced with the dilemma that once started, there is no option but to finish the task in a manner that is correct and perfect. Those first few paragraphs of a high-school essay become 'real' and therefore a public representation of the individual and what s/he can or cannot do. At such times, the fear of failure can become so strong that one must knuckle down and complete the task well *or* not go near it — all or nothing.

It would be incorrect to say that the young A/N person (child, teen, young adult) is comfortable with procrastination. They are more likely to be motivated by negative factors than by positive ones — to avoid failure, poor performance or being put into situations where the sense of self is at risk. Thus, for these people, time can be spent rehashing things multiple times so that the task is more or less complete before it is committed to the public arena. One of the traps for such people is that the more times they experience difficulties achieving at the level they believe is expected of them, the greater the fear of potential failure can become.

The developing internal driving force is to be correct, to be perfect or to not do the task at all. This is potentially contributed to by a sense of insecurity. The A/N person might not have grown up within a consistent framework where results, responses and affection were always predictable. The background to their development could have been one of high expectations — both external and then, over time, internal. The parenting style experienced may have involved restricted positive comments. It was therefore the shifting target for gaining approval that perhaps led to the insecurity around what is expected or appropriate. The level to be attained may have been unclear or even variable, which meant the child could only conceive of pushing hard/er in order to try to meet a target that was not specifically identified. An A in the last exam might lead to an expectation of an A+ in the next one, but with no greater level of resulting reinforcement. Acknowledgement from one or both parents might have been hard to obtain at times and approval possibly even more elusive. Without this, the child is at the mercy of external thresholds that can shift, though usually in the one direction: upwards. Alongside this, the parent's critical comments are internalized and this can become the predominant internal voice. However, it is now more powerful as it literally cannot be escaped and is also more undermining because it has become the 'self' telling the 'self' how poorly s/he is doing. It is of course a reflection of the critical parent but it is now someone who can be argued with even less — yourself.

Tolerating uncertainty

Slightly different to the above is a group of A/N people who have trouble tolerating uncertainty. One way this can come about is from early experience related to inconsistency in parental responses. Such inconsistency is perhaps more basic than the variable emotional availability described above. Some examples of this may relate to parenting difficulties exhibited by adults who lived with mood, anxiety or confidence problems. Unfortunately, a characteristic of such people and their struggles is variability in behaviour, which can result in their child being unable to predict how the parent might respond to the same behaviour at different times; the child therefore does not know how to behave or learn to identify what is an acceptable response to a task. This can have implications for developing confidence in handling ambiguous situations. In other situations, the adult behaviours can be somewhat chaotic, such that the structure of daily life can be compromised. An early life characterized by such issues can lead to the child seeking certainty and predictability, with a desire for things to be 'right' or 'just so'.

The other side of this is a difficulty tolerating the uncertainty inherent in daily life, because the early learning and developmental environment meant that few things were predictable. As a result, a sensitivity to issues and situations where expectations are not clear can develop. This tends to be managed by either withdrawal or learning to push oneself to reach the highest level which 'should' cover all possibilities regarding those expectations.

It is important to see that the developing need for certainty was functional (i.e. useful and real) at the time. Such learning is not easy to let go of, though, and it can quietly remain present then be triggered in future, similar circumstances. For the A/N individual, it can see them facing new challenges with an intolerance of, plus strong behavioural responses to, uncertain situations. In particular, these responses can be the tried and true behaviours of ignoring personal adversity, focusing on the task at hand in order to gain some control, and pushing themselves to overcome things. This issue of intolerance to uncertainty can be an important aspect of the A/N personality-style. Therefore, we will come back to this in more depth later.

· · · · · · · · · · · · · · · · · · · ·

As can be seen from this chapter, not everyone who has A/N traits came from exactly the same background. They may share some similarities in the factors that contributed to the way they interact with the world. However, it would be wrong to assume that any given A/N individual can be pigeon-holed as coming from one type of background or environment. I recall one client who provided a 'textbook' outline of A/N behaviours and the related longer-term impacts upon his personal wellbeing. As my therapist's antenna was triggered by the challenges he described, I offered the possibility that he had been raised within an environment with parents who had high standards and possibly even higher expectations of their children. To this insightful (I thought!) observation, he immediately replied, 'Not at all, Doc, my parents were both hippies; they didn't expect anything of us kids.' He went on to relate how he had consciously decided to establish personal standards, expect highly of himself and also push himself to achieve in reaction to this lack of expectation, structure and modelling. So, there are always variations on a theme. How you came to be living an A/N lifestyle may share similarities with a particular description from above or you might relate to components of several of these descriptions. Neither of these is wrong because, as you will see in this book, few things in this world are purely one thing or the other.

In order to manage this situation, the A/N adult can benefit from help to explore where the problems came from and how they developed. As part of this, it can be helpful for the A/N adult to realize that their internal pushing might be related to an early lack of acknowledgment and limited affirmation for success at any level other than 'being the best'. You might also benefit from understanding that there actually is such a thing as 'good enough' and that providing an outcome that is 'good enough' is not the lowest level of achievement, nor is it a failure. If there is no change in understanding or ability to manage this perfection driver, the child who becomes the A/N adult will continue to judge themselves harshly, feel they are underperforming (unless it is at the extreme end) and continue to push themselves.

IN SUMMARY

We don't tend to suddenly become an A/N individual, nor does it tend to come and go. Granted, we can all become focused on a project but the A/N personality-style is longer lasting than this. It possibly comes about within a family context with an orientation to achieving and performing well. The family may also have had at least one parent who lived these values and demonstrated, via their own behaviour, the way of approaching tasks. This modelling can be an important part of our earliest exposure to the ways of living life with an all-or-nothing attitude.

Related to the above, the way that significant others respond to your early behaviours has the ability to shape subsequent choices and actions. If you were praised for certain ways of behaving, you would be more likely to repeat those behaviours. Across time, as you encounter others who have similar approaches and standards, you will tend to carry on these ways of behaving. As a result, you perhaps come to expect that doing well and performing to high standards is what is required or 'usual'.

If our early environment was not consistent or we couldn't predict what was required to earn praise, we may have learnt to push ourselves in the hope of obtaining positive attention and reinforcement. One result of this is a sense that the outcome — as opposed to the process or effort — is the most important thing. This can become the yardstick for measuring our worth. If within the family praise and attention were tethered to high achievement, it is possible that we did not learn that 'good enough' is indeed good enough.

One risk with such a learning experience is that feeling good about your achievement can become externalized to the responses of and affirmations from others. The drive to achieve may have come from a need to please or measure up to other people but, over time, you might have taken on board the pressure to do well and to be seen as good. As much of the developing sense of self can depend on levels of achievement, a fear of failure can become a new 'driving' factor for important behaviours and tasks. This can lead to A/N people seeing the world in an either/or manner, whereby we are either meeting the high standards we set ourselves or we are failing.

As the young person (and developing A/N individual) has little practice with realistic and fair expectations, the only choice seems to be to push oneself in order to meet the goal/s that have been set. Unfortunately, along with this drive to achieve can come a strong tendency to judge (read: criticize!) yourself and your performance.

ASPECTS FOR REFLECTION, OPTIONS FOR CHANGE

Developing an understanding of where things come from doesn't mean that blame needs to be assigned. This is not about saying 'This is Mum's/Dad's fault' and then feeling absolved of responsibility. Nor is it about becoming angry at 'them' for doing 'this' to 'me'. Rather, it is more about understanding, learning and realizing why things came about. If you can gain this appreciation, then things might not seem so random and perhaps there is more potential for gaining some control. If you are tempted to apportion blame, remember that one or more of your parents might have exhibited some of these A/N behaviours and . . . guess where they might have got it from? Chances are that they picked up their approach to life in much the same way that you have — via modelling, reinforcement and shaping of responses to situations.

From this chapter, you have hopefully gained some idea of how your A/N approach to life may have developed. If you can also get a handle on what has been maintaining this A/N approach, you may feel in a stronger position to bring about some change. Therefore the next chapter will consider a range of factors that may have kept the A/N approach alive for you. Hopefully, if you can gain an understanding of these factors, you may be open to considering whether there are new or different ways of engaging in activities that can help you shift from the patterns of behaviour that have become so familiar.

Try this

Although there are further aspects to explore and learn about an A/N approach to life, one question to consider as you continue to read this book is whether things have to remain this way forever. Maybe, just maybe, it might be all right to pause and ask yourself if it is okay at this stage of your life to consider doing things differently. In this vein, complete the following simple statements. You might not come up with any answers immediately, or you might even come up with reasons why this won't work. If so, don't panic. This doesn't mean that considering something new is wrong or impossible. Chances are that you are experiencing your mind throwing up the barriers to change — it doesn't like moving away from the familiar and can easily generate many reasons for remaining with the status quo. Don't be put off by this; just have another go.

Complete the following sentences in your own words.

If I finished work earlier each night I would be able to . . .

_____

_____

_____

By having more time with my partner/family, my life would . . .

_____

_____

_____

When I learn to be less hard on myself, it will be easier to . . .

_____

_____

_____

Not expecting myself to be perfect will allow me to . . .

_____

_____

_____

3 What keeps this all going?

As we have seen, there is a flow on from early learning and life experiences through to our behaviour and responses as a young person and then as an adult. This ties together the connections between parenting, family dynamics and expectations as well as the reinforcement paradigms we encounter over time.

These important variables come together in an individual 'soup' that is specific to each person and will be expressed in ways dependent on the person, their history, the relevant environment and social situation. It may also be that these variables have a bearing on what professional roles we seek out in adult life, the types of sports we favour and artistic endeavours we embark upon. Although these situations may present new learning experiences and have a range of demands, it is likely that what we bring may have a key role in determining how we engage, how we succeed and, importantly, how long we can sustain something for. Thus, it might not be what we do but how we do it that is most relevant!

SCHEMAS: YOUR PRE-GOOGLE GUIDANCE SYSTEM

Engagement in activity is not a simple relationship of 'see task, do task'. There is a multitude of variables within the individual that can come into play. These include the person's immediate appraisal of the situation and the actual decisions taken. From these, the behaviour will follow in response; this can be a new or novel approach or an automatic behaviour. Underpinning an automatic behaviour are longstanding and often deeply entrenched determiners of behaviour, also known as schemas. These are beliefs or ways of viewing the world that have been laid down and reinforced over a number of years. In essence, schemas serve as templates to help us make sense of events, plus they impact how we think about and approach our world.

Over time, our schemas affect how we view ourselves, and they impact both our activity and our relationships with others. Additionally, they will begin to influence choices around behaviour. Importantly, schemas, once laid down, are very hard to rid ourselves of. The problem, however, may not be that the schemas are present or activated, but that we put them into action frequently and rigidly. This is of relevance to the A/N individual, who tends to repeatedly and unquestioningly apply the early messages about effort, achievement and what is required to be 'good' (or should that be perfect?) at something.

CASE STUDY

When I first met Selena she held a responsible position as a personal assistant to a senior manager. She had been referred for help with chronic pain from an injury. As we explored the impact of her injury, it became clear that Selena had significant challenges with pacing her activity levels — she overdid things consistently. It also became clear that she was experiencing difficulties with sleeping and described herself as 'run down'. At work, Selena was a busy, efficient and very capable assistant — a fact that had become known to many people in the organization.

Unfortunately, Selena had also become a victim of her own success. Colleagues and managers outside of her team regularly came to her with problems and difficulties that they could not sort out. One of the biggest difficulties for Selena was in placing boundaries around her workload, and she regularly stayed beyond her finishing time to complete her work (as she had prioritized other people's during the day). After a long commute home, Selena would prepare the evening meal for her family and then attend to any issues and needs of her loved ones. This pattern inevitably took until bedtime, and Selena described being unable to wind down as she was already mentally preparing for the next day's tasks.

It transpired that Selena came from a family where both parents worked full-time. Her role had been to care for the younger children and essentially be responsible for their welfare and upbringing while her parents made the money for the family. Selena described that she felt strong pressures to ensure her siblings behaved well, did their homework and had ironed clothes each day — in essence, she was given an adult role at a young age and she took this responsibility very seriously. When I asked Selena what the parental expectations of her were, she replied: 'To be caring, to keep the peace, to help out, to be good and to do what I was asked.'

The schemas or core beliefs A/N people respond to can be around working hard, being the best, looking after others or not showing weakness. They tend to lie dormant until activated by a situation that is familiar, or by a combination of factors and events that conspire to trigger them. (This is much the same process that allows a dormant virus to express itself.) Perhaps a key issue is that, once a schema is kicked into gear, it will open a box that contains familiar and well-rehearsed behaviours. There is an interaction between the individual person (with all his/her prior experiences and beliefs) and the situation. However, there tends to be little appraisal of the situation that is confronting the individual or of the range of options available at the time. Rather, there will usually be a response that is connected to feelings, thoughts and behaviours the person has previously employed in similar situations. Without the appraisal aspect (where we make sense of things), there is an automatic implementation of the relevant schema and this will continue to be the case in future (similar) events and situations.

In some ways, the schemas act as a sort of shorthand that guide us and almost pre-select behaviours for situations. Think of them as being a bit like Mother Nature's version of Google Maps: a course of action is put forward without much actual thinking having been applied, and then we follow it. However, without accounting for variations to the situation or suggested route, we can sometimes end up in an environment that we are not fully prepared for. This is much like the news reports of hapless travellers who blindly trust their mapping device only to find themselves in the middle of nowhere, up a goat track (unable to reverse down) with snow falling, daylight disappearing and only an already opened can of Coke and half-eaten egg sandwich for company. Not quite what they had planned or expected when they set out on a course of action.

It is true that using schemas can be very adaptive and labour saving, but some of the schemas may not have been developed in the most supportive of environments. Thus, they can contain and promote responses that can cost us in the long run. With respect to A/N behaviour, the messages we have been given by significant others and the expectations we have taken on board often impact how we view activities, roles and tasks. Our early life-events lay the groundwork for the schemas, which will then be triggered in situations related to performance. As a result, the A/N individual will potentially respond in a manner that follows the script associated with pushing, achieving and doing their best.

Bamber and McMahon (2008) suggest that individuals are drawn unconsciously to situations, and therefore employment choices, that will trigger the not-always-helpful schemas they developed early on (e.g. don't stop a task until everything is complete). Additionally, the authors suggest that certain underlying schemas may actually be a vulnerability factor for developing occupational stress later in life (e.g. burn-out). They go on to say that healthcare workers often have strong schemas around caring for others which may have begun as a way to gain approval within the family environment. This 'self-sacrifice' schema is identified as coming at the cost of not prioritizing or meeting their own needs. Bamber and McMahon also give examples of another early schema associated with perfectionistic behaviours and the drive to meet high personal standards. They relate this type of schema to growing up in an environment with strong expectations and not much flexibility within the parental and familial expectations. As such, the researchers seem to be supporting the ideas put forward in Chapter 2. One of the most interesting aspects of Bamber and McMahon's work is around the notion that while the unhelpful schemas can sometimes have a negative impact as you live with them, they may also be central to your ability to perform in a quality manner. The writers go on to offer the seemingly ironic viewpoint that these same (potentially unhelpful) ways of interacting with the world may actually have positive spin-offs for the organization, industry or sporting worlds that the individual engages in. A real-life example of this is illustrated in the case study of Selena (see p. 47). Thus, the needs of the individual (over time) might not be met but the needs of the group or organization may well be met or exceeded.

In order to make gains and positive changes for your life, you might need to account for what is happening behind the scenes. It is not enough to just identify the unhelpful behaviours (e.g. consistently working long hours or redoing work to achieve perfection). Change will only be enduring if you can learn about the schemas that are pushing you to act in potentially unhelpful and/or unhealthy ways. By understanding and formulating what is behind the rigidly enacted behaviours plus the costs attached, there is more chance the A/N individual can understand and see merit in the effort required to bring about change and then sustain it.

PERSONALITY-STYLE: THE 'YOU' AND HOW YOU SHOW THIS

It is important that we do not make the mistake of relating to personality-styles — the way you action or demonstrate the elements of who you are — as being complete and total. It can be more helpful to understand that the A/N person might have a number of strengths and weaknesses and that these can, in turn, be comprised of a range of 'sub-species'. An important element is the tendency to be conscientious, which the industrial and organizational psychology literature identifies as a key variable related to performance with tasks. However, it may well be that there are sub-components to this important aspect. We should therefore be asking what makes up this conscientious behaviour. If we can identify these aspects, there may be more opportunity to finetune the impact and expression of this. Some of the key ingredients within this conscientious approach to work life include a sense of duty, an all-encompassing orientation towards achievement and of course some pretty strong willpower or self-discipline. By accounting for these factors, we may be able to bring about a more fine-grained analysis of the individual's life, patterns of behaviour and repeated actions which, in turn, can offer more specific targets for change and modification.

It is possible that, by the decisions taken and behaviours expressed, a person may be shaping their world to some extent. The personality-style brought to the workplace and demonstrated within that environment may well promote particular behaviours and ways of engaging in relationships. Evidence of this can be seen in choices of specialty areas within the medical world. Any patient who has undergone surgery can readily tell you there is a plain and obvious difference in personality and 'bedside manner' between the family doctor, the anaesthetist and the surgeon (ever tried getting one of the latter to converse with you for more than 6 minutes?). It is also true that people who like to push themselves and value achievement are seldom likely to undertake roles whose goals are easily met and provide no challenge. This is as valid within the sporting and artistic fields as it is in the business world. By choosing jobs that fit with their personal disposition, a person may demonstrate greater job performance (they like it, so will do more) and this will probably lead to job-related success.

It is, of course, too simplistic to say that personality-style drives everything. As with any batch of cocktails, the quantities, flavour and relative strengths of each constituent will have a bearing on the brew that results, what the dominant taste may be . . . and the eventual outcome. Think about your favourite cocktail or mixed drink; now consider the difference in taste, pleasurable experience and after-effect of that same drink mixed by a professional in a cocktail lounge and a batch made up at a university students' party! Similarly, in terms of job performance, there may well be an interactive effect between the personality-style, job chosen, workplace setting and general environmental factors associated with the individual's world. Remember that what you personally bring to the role will interact with any training or learning you undergo within that employment situation. The question, of course, is whether one can alter a key 'ingredient', eliminate it (or its effect) or perhaps attempt to provide ways of softening the way it is experienced. Thus, with personality-styles, the goal might not be to eliminate a certain aspect but rather to learn how much (and when) to dial it in or out. This is based on the fact that aspects of personality are not entirely positive or entirely negative; perhaps the degree, frequency and strength with which they are expressed may be more relevant.

Understanding yourself

Rather than attempting a 'personality-ectomy', it might be best to understand where your specific vulnerabilities are, to recognize when your schemas are becoming active and know how to manage or mitigate their effect. Potentially, greater change and gains can be brought about by understanding (and working with) your personality-style. Key to helping this be acceptable is to understand that having a strong and goal-focused personality-style is not wrong. Rather, it is about understanding the at-times problematic aspects and identifying why it might be useful to be able to modify the impact of the behaviours that follow. This can offer a useful outline or framework from whence to begin making change — not 'all or nothing' change but, rather, a finetuning that might provide benefits to you, your health and career.

INTOLERANCE OF UNCERTAINTY

Given that some A/N individuals have come from an environment characterized by not knowing what is expected of them, such people may have difficulties tolerating events and situations which are not clearly defined. The A/N person prefers to know what is expected, how to participate and also (possibly most importantly) what the threshold is for achievement. Coming from a family or developmental environment where things were not always predictable can lead to problems handling situations that are not clear. How does one set their sights or apportion energy if the requirements are not outlined? Not being sure about things can lead to a person interpreting such situations as threatening. Indeed, ambiguity can be a scary place for the A/N person to be. Without specifics, it is hard to set goals and know how much effort to expend. This ambiguity can potentially set up a sense of dread, particularly around the potential for performing poorly. The chances of failure may actually be low but, unfortunately, the probabilities are not always identified in a realistic manner.

Intolerance of uncertainty is essentially a way of viewing the world and, more specifically, events that are personally important. The individual develops or maintains a sort of bias in the way they view things — with an emphasis on the negative. It is about relating to current or future events as potentially threatening, even if there is no clear evidence that things will go wrong. As a result, the person can start to behave in ways that might reduce this uncertainty. They may seek increasing amounts of detail from others (e.g. supervisors or colleagues) as a way of bringing about some clarity. This is aimed at making themselves feel safer and more confident by attempting to impose some structure on events. However, it can have unintended negative effects; for example, within the workplace people can view your reassurance-seeking as an admission of inability.

Mahoney and McEvoy, in a 2011 article, suggest that being intolerant of uncertainty sets one up for a difficult time, by making it uncomfortable and challenging to encounter situations where things cannot be predicted or outcomes assured. The latter taps into the perfectionistic drives within the A/N person and sets in process a chain of events that can undermine confidence, promote negative anticipation and bring about possible avoidance (e.g. procrastination).

Tolerating uncertainty is a multidimensional experience. It involves, cognitive, emotional and behavioural responses to the uncertainty, all of which are characterized by an unpleasant gnawing sensation. Remember that the A/N person has been striving for a long time to be in control of situations; when faced with uncertainty, the sense of self is at risk and the person may start to feel vulnerable. Unfortunately, this can be interpreted within oneself as weakness (Harsh Internal Critic, anyone?), which of course can be further threatening to personal identity. Within this context, the person may respond in a manner that biases interpretations and general processing towards the worst-case scenario. Consider what this is like if your role is to make policy decisions or offer advice to other departments within an organization.

It perhaps is not hard to see how this difficulty around tolerating uncertainty develops within the A/N person. In essence, uncertainty relates to the potential for things to go wrong (e.g. poor outcomes) — this clashes with the internal image, and demands of the person to be in control and always achieving. Coupled with a harsh inner critic, such a self-image can cause a degree of dissonance: key things about the self do not fit together too well. Anticipatory concerns therefore clash with the positive, 'in control' self-perception that usually drives the person towards achievement. Both perfectionism and the tendency to overthink things can then lead to a 'paralysis by analysis', where the person struggles to think clearly, making decisions or actions based on an overfocus on detail or certain facets of a task. This results in the person feeling as though they can't function (or function to the expected standard) when faced with uncertainty. This can become an even greater issue if deadlines are looming and strict.

Mahoney and McEvoy suggest that intolerance of uncertainty may be most apparent and relevant in relation to environments of core concern. While the person may be struggling generally to tolerate uncertainty, this can become even more pronounced in, for example, the office or boardroom; overestimating the potential for negative outcomes can become a major problem when operating at levels of high responsibility where peak performance is central to maintaining your standards and position. A key issue here is about the negative estimation and unfortunately, over time this way of viewing situations can become an automatic process, which makes it hard to identify and therefore manage. Once this process is set in train, however, it flows towards the perfection driver and starts to raise some concerns about performance and therefore outcome. The internal critic then comes in to bat and may well change the course and direction of the game. Initially, this may mean a doubling of effort to overcome the perceived challenges, but it may also lead to the fear of failure taking over and impacting the chosen responses.

However, the issue to grasp here is that there may actually be no real basis for the threatening view. Therefore, the negative tailspin that eventuates may be unnecessary. As a result, confidence levels may also be unnecessarily affected. When all this is operating, the person might become 'paralyzed' due to the uncertainty, so that they find it hard to make decisions or put relevant actions into place. Thus, a previously decisive and efficient individual may well find they can no longer perform in the manner accustomed or expected. If they are someone the team looks to for direction and decisions, such hesitation may become obvious and impact team morale and trust.

From this we can see that a lowering of performance may be related to the A/N individual's strong need for predictability (with its associated sense of comfort and confidence) and the resulting paralysis that comes from the uncertainty they struggle with. Such a combination can lead to catastrophizing (about the task, personal performance and future) and this can flow on to increased worry. But what if you could learn that uncertainty is not a portent of doom? What if it could be seen as something that can be tolerated and even managed? The outcome would be the chance to continue succeeding, which may also help stave off some of the unhelpful self-doubts that can eat away at you from time to time.

IN SUMMARY

As this chapter has made clear, there are thinking processes that happen before a behaviour or activity occurs. The pattern is as follows:

Perspective

↓

Appraisal

↓

Decisions and choices

↓

Behaviours, taking action

Despite these thinking process being intangible, they are nevertheless real and are key components to how things develop. Generally, we can easily notice the final phase of taking action. However, the steps prior to this are what orient the individual and prime them for responding in certain ways. Importantly, the perspective one brings to a situation can direct the flow of traffic, so to speak. The next step is appraisal, or how we make sense of what is in front of us at any given time. Both these aspects can be influenced by a range of things, such as mood state or environmental demands. The other aspect we are now aware of is the role of schemas, which may lie underneath these processes and consistently influence them. Thus, to truly bring about a better understanding of what is driving a behaviour (e.g. working relentlessly) we need to take account of all these factors.

Schemas provide us with a shorthand way for making sense of the world. They develop within our early, personal environment and influence how we interact with the world. However, problems stem from how we put schemas into practice. We tend to run with them without thinking, due to the fact they are so familiar. One result of this is that we repeatedly use the same responses to situations and may rigidly follow the 'guidelines' offered by the schemas. However, if we can become more flexible in how we make sense of situations and explore options for responding, we will have a better chance of adapting to tasks.

For A/N people, any lack of clarity is a scary zone to be playing around in. Uncertainty is seen as threatening and therefore something to be avoided, but experience shows us that this is not always possible. The feelings of threat can lead to a reduced sense of confidence and tug at the need for perfection while simultaneously undermining the sense of self. Unfortunately, over time, uncertainty in life can affect how a person relates to their role, colleagues and specific tasks. This changed approach is characterized by a negative estimation of the threat value, which results in the risks being over-identified — which in turn can lead to a triggering of the fear of failure.

ASPECTS FOR REFLECTION, OPTIONS FOR CHANGE

Difficulties tolerating uncertainty revolve around worry about the future, so it can be helpful to become more comfortable with the 'here and now'. What might life be like if you learnt to adopt more of a 'wait and see' attitude, rather than chasing the goal of wanting to control every uncertain situation? You might find it becomes easier to live in a space where not everything is predictable, for, in essence, isn't this what life is actually like? One key aspect to making a change like this is to view problems and setbacks as simply a normal part of life. Now here's a bit of a mind-spin for you: what if these uncertain situations could be viewed as opportunities to learn or refine your technique, or develop new ways of approaching a task?

There can be a strong drive to avoid uncertain situations. However, you may have gathered already that such avoidance does not teach you anything about managing either the situations themselves or the associated feelings. One approach to help address this is to consciously put yourself in situations where you start to feel uncertain and therefore uncomfortable. '*What?*' I hear you scream . . . Be bold and do something really scary, such as being spontaneous! Consider doing something on the spur of the moment — radical, I know! This doesn't have to be a major task or accomplishment; it can be heading out to buy something (unplanned) for dinner, going out to visit something or someone (not tomorrow or next week but *today*), sitting down to listen to your favourite music this afternoon (just because you like it) or going for a drive to the beach or park (for no reason other than the weather is nice). Try to incorporate such spontaneity into your life on a more regular basis.

The aim is to confront and open yourself up to situations that will provoke a sense of uncertainty. Show yourself that there doesn't always need to be a reason or goal associated with doing things. With these tasks, the risks are small but they will still bring about feelings of uncertainty (partly because there is no script and therefore no predictable outcome) and if you face these feelings, you are on the way to overcoming them. You can gently and gradually extend the level and type of spontaneity to differing domains in your life if you like. This will expose you (in a controlled manner, with few major consequences) to the discomfort and will help inoculate you to the unsettling impact of the emotional responses, such as feeling exposed and out of control.

In order to help with the long-standing need for predictability, it can help to become more accepting of the feelings associated with uncertainty. Part of this is to realize that at times such feelings are essentially unavoidable and are, for the most part, harmless (uncomfortable, for sure, but still harmless). First, though, you will need to know when you are experiencing these feelings of uncertainty and become aware of the unhelpful thoughts and feelings that accompany them. Try the following simple exercise, for which you'll need a pen and paper.

Try this

Think about a role or task that you were unexpectedly asked to complete by someone such as a supervisor or boss at work, your coach at training or your best friend in a social setting. Take yourself back to the moment you were asked to do this and think about what began to run through your mind . . . what were the very first thoughts? These are not the detailed appraisal or risk analysis you performed later on but, rather, your immediate thoughts upon hearing the task described. What do you recall about how you began to feel (emotionally and physically) in those first few seconds and minutes? Now write down those thoughts, physical sensations and emotional feelings. What do you notice about them? How would you describe the 'flavour' of these thoughts and feelings? Is there a theme running through them?

If you notice that the feelings and thoughts relate to being unsure (about your ability, for example, or the outcome or what people will think of you), have another go at the above task but use a different scenario and see if the patterns repeat themselves. This of course requires you to be honest with yourself about the thoughts and feelings. Remember, there is no one to impress here, only a person being open to identifying patterns and possibly learning how to deal with aspects that may be keeping fears and concerns alive. If being anxious or unsure is the theme, then revisit each of your scenarios but this time, focus on breathing calmly in a relaxed manner and allow yourself to see that these feelings and thoughts can be tolerated and they don't have to result in avoidance or poor performance.

· · · · · · · · · · · · · · · · · · · ·

To end this chapter, reflect on the following words of wisdom (author unknown):

Ain't no use worrying about things beyond your control,
Because if they're beyond your control, ain't no use worrying . . .
Ain't no use worrying about things within your control,
Because if you have them under control, ain't no use worrying.

4 Avoiding things and then . . . the 'nothing'

Intriguingly, the 'nothing' part of 'all or nothing' is rarely discussed. A lot is said about the 'all' part — total participation and pushing oneself. So, why is the second part less understood and, in my experience, therefore not addressed?

In part, it seems that the 'nothing' aspect is often accepted as simply being the end result of the 'all' phase; that the tank has run dry and there is simply no gas left to continue with goals and aims. Although there is some truth in this, I would suggest that this is not the whole answer. Indeed, by minimizing what is involved, we may be missing an important opportunity to understand (and then assist) the person whose life is characterized by the all-or-nothing approach. Therefore, a central issue to consider may be: what promotes certain key behaviours exhibited by the A/N person? Are these people solely motivated to achieve, or could they also be driven by a desire to *avoid* potential outcomes or consequences of their actions? On the surface, it appears quite obvious that the A/N person is keen to make gains and build on achievements. While this may be true up to a point, what if there are other forces at work, which promote certain ways of responding yet are not so readily identifiable or detected?

This chapter examines how the 'nothing' aspect may have come about plus why it remains a part of the individual's decision making. It will soon become clear that there is not one simple or universal explanation for this 'nothing' behaviour. However, it may be equally true that some readers of this book experience more than one 'reason' for this aspect of their personality-style. By highlighting the potential reasons, it is hoped that the individual may be better placed to bring about sustainable change.

CASE STUDY

Being a stockbroker can be an exciting and stimulating role. Terry had built up a track record of identifying shares that had potential for good gains and his clients certainly appreciated this. Within the firm, he received both recognition and reward. However, he eventually found that even talented and skilled people can get things wrong. Following some not-so-successful choices and recommendations, this experienced broker developed a crisis of confidence. As he told it to me,

Terry started to find it difficult to make decisions as quickly and incisively as before. He noticed himself holding back from starting the reports that were expected and some weren't being completed. We identified that he was concerned his superiors might find fault, judge him and consider he was no longer up to the task.

Unfortunately, Terry's confidence suffered further when the inevitable questions did come regarding the lateness of reports. In order to keep himself 'safe' from such judgments, Terry began avoiding interactions with colleagues and, eventually, he found it threatening and anxiety provoking to answer his phone or open emails — which are important tools of his trade. Due to his declining performance, Terry was asked to step aside for a time and take 'stress leave'.

WHAT'S BEHIND THE 'NOT DOING'?

The classic and most obvious explanation for doing 'nothing' is that the A/N person is so focused on the task at hand that they simply have no time available for engaging in complementary or previously undertaken activities. By spending long hours at work and utilizing your spare time to sort out associated issues, you have probably found there is little time to do other activities. It is this stark contrast that tends to bring about the observation that A/N people do only one thing and have no time for anything else. Such an understanding is undoubtedly correct for many, and it is often a partner or family members who most often observe this apparent lack of interest for engaging in any other activities.

Another possible contributing factor to ceasing involvement in a task is that the person may have simply run out of energy. This is potentially a direct result of the full-on approach to tasks that tends to involve long hours of activity, commitment and focus. It is often observed and suggested that the level of interest and available energy has ended simply because such people have run themselves into the ground. Therefore, the A/N person just stops what they are doing and does not return to it, even though the task might not be complete. Such ceasing of involvement sits in clear contrast to the usual outcome of achieving the goal, and therefore tends to put the spotlight on the change in direction and motivation. This different outcome — not finishing versus all done and completed — seems strange given the person's history. Anecdotally (and clinically) there would seem to be a good level of evidence for this possible explanation; see, for example, the case studies of Matthew (p. 3) and Jason (p. 16) whom we met earlier. It may be that people, like you, can become physically unwell due to the high degree of activity or elevated stress levels they have been operating under. Additionally, such people may experience burn-out in relation to their job or become depressed or anxious as a result of pushing themselves (physically and cognitively) over an extended period. These latter issues would seem to be particularly relevant for A/N people and we will therefore come back to them in more detail in a later chapter.

Doing 'nothing' is not an absence of goals or motivation. Nor is it simply a result of laziness. What seems like the abandoning of a project — at times in a serial manner — can, for some people, be related to a fear of being judged. As A/N individuals progress with the task at hand, the well-identified approach of shutting out the rest of the world is followed. However, as some people close in on the end of the project, a fear of it not being good enough or up to the 'required' standard may take hold. The threat of being judged by others can also come into play, which can result in abandonment of the project in an effort to avoid the sense of embarrassment associated with producing an inferior (in their mind) product or outcome. Approaching the end of a project means our performance is about to become public and therefore may be open to scrutiny. Not wishing to be seen as second-rate, or not as good as our image, has always been suggested as a powerful driver for some A/N people. It can see them ceasing their engagement in the task and perhaps not wishing to undertake another activity that will result in the same threat.

The A/N person will often push, via their tenacious nature, to try to overcome obstacles. However, despite their best efforts there may come a point when things are not working out but energy is still being expended, and then it is time to pull back from the task. But is this 'giving up' or is the behaviour motivated by avoidance? Stopping an activity or project may be related to the need to avoid failing or, worse, looking incompetent in the eyes of valued colleagues, employers or others whose opinion matters. The latter is crucially important for many A/N individuals, as negative feedback is taken on board strongly and seen as real-life evidence that they did not possess the abilities required for the role. I have repeatedly been amazed in my clinical practice at how capable and highly achieving people can have a gnawing doubt around their ability and capability.

Self-efficacy

By now you are probably getting the sense that A/N people have a tendency to focus on performance and attaining the goal or outcome. Unfortunately, if your identity is built upon achieving goals, this sense of self may become vulnerable when confronted with challenges and potential failure. If one struggles to meet a self-set goal and fails then, surely, this *must* mean (note the absolute style of thinking here) that they do not possess the strengths, abilities or characteristics they hoped were part of their make-up. If confidence is predicated upon continued achievement, that confidence may falter when progress slows and achievement is not able to be brought about. This perhaps strikes at the very building block of progress and achievement: self-efficacy.

The concept of self-efficacy comes from the field of social psychology and revolves around a person's belief that they can bring about a certain outcome within a particular context. Generally speaking, this relates to a sense that they can complete a given task despite the challenges they may face. It is important to realize that this isn't about skill level or knowledge but rather the appraisal one makes of how they might perform on a given task or in a given situation. A relatively intact sense of self-efficacy is therefore necessary for attempting and successfully completing tasks. Conversely, if the degree of self-efficacy is reducing or already low, the individual would be more likely to not continue with the task or 'give up' i.e. the 'nothing' part of our descriptor.

This important building block of achievement is not one of those things that a person either has or does not have. There is some suggestion in the literature that people have different levels of positive belief around their ability to do things (high to low self-efficacy) and, additionally, this belief within each individual may not be the same across all situations encountered. Interestingly, there also seems to be an effect whereby a person will perform at higher levels if important others (e.g. managers at work or sporting coaches) are confident that the person can meet the grade or do the task that's presented to them. However, Lunenburg (2011) discusses some research that points out that the level of this effect or positive impact may be related to the manager's credibility, their previous relationship with the employee and their influence in the organization.

For our purposes, this issue could have relevance for the A/N person's developing (and possibly variable) sense of self-efficacy. If a key person such as a parent or authority figure (see Chapter 2) encourages the young person and expresses faith in their ability, it may help the developing sense of self-efficacy but if the relationship with the parent is fraught with difficulties or uncertainties, the sense of self-efficacy may not be as complete or robust as it might otherwise have been. This may subsequently be expressed as a variable level of self-efficacy that is intact up to a point, but which lessens or even dissolves when challenges are encountered, potentially leading to what we see as the 'nothing' aspect of behaviour.

FEARFUL? SURELY NOT

As discussed earlier, people with an all-or-nothing personality-style often harbour an underlying fear that they may fail at the task before them, either in terms of observable outcomes or a sense that they have not met their own targets. It is generally accepted that most people push themselves so that they can achieve. However, conversely, this pushing could also be framed as a way of not encountering failure, of avoiding the negative feelings and knowledge that one did not meet the goal, whether short, medium or longer term. The latter is perhaps the most pertinent for A/N people.

Although it may seem as if we are splitting hairs, what if A/N individuals are not purely motivated by achievement but are also driven by a fear of being confronted by failure and thus a need to avoid it? As you will recall from Chapter 2, a key aspect in the development of the A/N approach of pushing oneself can be the expectations of parental figures. Such important early figures may make it clear that failure is not acceptable — yet, ironically, the criteria for what constitutes failure might not have been clearly defined. Perhaps most important for our consideration are the verbal responses to a performance which does not meet parental expectation. The language used can be less than positive and sometimes derogatory, leaving the listener in no doubt that they did not accomplish what was required of them. Almost by definition, by not meeting the expected outcome one has failed. It therefore isn't hard to see how this becomes an aversive state of affairs. If positive reinforcement and attention are withheld and the feedback is less than positive, a young person can easily become fearful of encountering this outcome again. No matter what is produced, things could have been better. Or at least this is the message received from significant others who are expecting the high-level outcomes. For some, this may grow into a fear of looking bad or not measuring up — of becoming a failure.

Lack of meaning

As noted in Chapter 2, the A/N personality-style can be related, to a greater or lesser degree, to an upbringing where consistency was not demonstrated. This can result in the developing individual being unsure where to set their goals, and without some guidelines as to what is acceptable it can be hard to generate a sense of meaningfulness in life. This can see an A/N person pushing themself hard and throwing themself into an activity or task, but gaining no sense of fulfilment. Despite the hard slog and the intense focus, it can start to become clear that 'this' (whatever it is) is not what you are looking for.

This sense of uncertainty and lack of meaningful connection can result in arriving at a personal crossroads (cue images from a host of philosophical, existential or horror movies — your choice) where it is deemed better to stop the current activity because it does not seem to be providing what is sought. As a result, the person ceases the task and enters a period of inactivity, which is characterized by a sense of disillusionment and 'What's the point?'. Such a phase is not necessarily due to lowered mood but more around the fact that the sense of self was wrapped up in the outcome and achievement aspects of the project; that is, feeling good depends upon achieving a very good outcome. Interestingly, this phase of 'nothing' does not always last long. The person, whose personal identity has taken a bit of a hammering, may soon seek a new project and throw themselves into it so that they can retrieve some feelings of self-worth and hopefully head towards some meaningfulness within their life. Due to the fact that the personal identity is closely related to achievement, a see-saw effect can develop whereby this pattern is repeated over time.

Conditional confidence

Although A/N individuals seem to be confident and positive, this may (for some, at least) be a conditional thing. When they are on target and moving towards their goals, such people tend to be motivated, focused and positive about why they are doing a task and also the fact it will be achieved. However, some people can also have problems with procrastination, which could be related to avoidance. The perfection driver kicks in and makes it hard to start a task or project for fear that it won't be good enough. This fear undermines productivity and can bring about clashes with timeframes and therefore efficiency. This of course can heighten the fear of failure that was underlying the process initially, and can also bring up doubts about one's potential to perform the task. This can be further impacted if the target or timeframes are missed.

At such times, any negative comments from colleagues or bosses tend to be interpreted as 'proof' that the person does not have the required ability. However, there can also be a reactive aspect within this, perhaps one that occurs prior to the ceasing of the activity. The person can enter a phase where they push themselves harder — even to exhaustion or breaking point — to try to achieve the goal that seems to be slipping from their grasp. The main drive now becomes one of avoidance — in this case, it may be around avoiding appearing incompetent to an employer or team leader.

. . . .

Hopefully, you can now see that the 'nothing' aspect of life for an A/N person isn't just about giving up. There may well be complex reasons why this approach has come about. In particular, the fear of failure seems to be implicated and this can promote avoidance-type behaviours where you do not go near, may not start or will not finish certain tasks in order to avoid encountering something that is aversive to you. The aversive threat (public embarrassment or negative judgment by an important person) is often perceived as potentially overwhelming by the A/N individual, *even if the actual threat is minimal.* It is not always understood by the A/N person, or indeed their employer, just how strong this fear of performing badly can be. The resulting 'nothing' behaviour is not just a cop out. Rather, it is a powerful and ever present aspect of the personality-style that can determine how you engage with life. As such, the stopping of an activity may not be a well thought-out plan. The person might actually be responding to an unconscious drive that is fuelled by a fear they did not even realize was part of them. If an individual can avoid a negative experience, then the stopping or 'nothing' aspect may actually feel comfortable. It can also be safer for their sense of self to be able to say that they did not try rather than be confronted with a judgment that they weren't up to par.

MISSED OPPORTUNITIES FOR LEARNING

For the A/N person raised in an unpredictable environment, there is little opportunity to see that not achieving can be a chance to learn or finetune. If failure is something to be avoided at all costs, there is the real risk that the focus fixes solely on the outcome and not the process. Within the execution of tasks, there can be multiple opportunities to see where behaviour and responses can be shaped to bring about a different outcome. This allows people to see where they might benefit from some adjustment, and provides a learning environment that permits experimentation and (ultimately) tolerance of setbacks. However, if failure is so aversive, there is a narrowing of focus which skips over these learning opportunities and gets bogged down in the outcome: 'I passed' or 'I failed'. There is no grey area, no meritorious effort, just a feeling of 'I didn't quite get there'.

With respect to avoidance, it is possible that some A/N people may not closely monitor their progress with projects. There are of course clear exceptions to this: think of marathon runners who prepare for extended periods and religiously record all aspects of their training. If reduced monitoring occurs, however, it may not necessarily represent a laissez-faire attitude. Rather, it can indicate a fear of encountering signs or feedback that the current (or potential) performance is not up to scratch. Worse still, it increases focus upon the difference between what one expects of oneself and the actual performance being achieved. This is an unhelpful characteristic of some A/N people in that they tend to take the 'negative' feedback (even if it is a progress update) as a *fait accompli*, rather than seeing it as an opportunity to alter and adapt. Avoidance of monitoring or checking in on performance becomes an important part of salvaging some positive sense of self. That is: if I don't check on things then there will be no indication that I am 'failing'. Although this approach is clearly less than helpful from a learning and adjustment perspective, it makes some sense to a person with a vulnerability around their beliefs on achievement.

A challenge for the A/N person is to learn to tolerate errors, failure or poor performance. There may have been little room in your early life for tolerating, let alone accepting, a performance that was not up to scratch. Due to the aforementioned learning environments, you may have never been given (or given yourself) the permission to be 'bad' at something. As a result, you are able to identify potential 'failure' from a great distance but do not necessarily recognize this lesser outcome for what it could be: a chance to learn something, either about yourself or your performance.

A/N people do not build up the resilience to less-than-perfect performances as they do not see this as part of normal, everyday life, as most others on the planet do. Perhaps what is needed is to be able to appraise one's effort rather than just the outcome. This can help you to see there is a process involved and that this can be adjusted or finetuned, not just passed or failed. Don't forget that a fundamental error for A/N people is to see the result as the whole picture rather than part of a process. In fact, for such people, it really is about the end result alone. Due to the strong negative associations with poor or under-performance, there are always powerful and unsettling memories that will surface and maintain the drive to avoid doing poorly. As mentioned above, addressing the 'nothing' part of the person's world may not be as simple as stopping a behaviour or not engaging in their 'usual' approach any more.

IN SUMMARY

Part of getting a good handle on the A/N approach to life is understanding all aspects of it. The 'all' part is easy to grasp but the 'nothing' aspect is often neglected or misunderstood. Some behaviours can actually be in order to avoid potentially negative or feared outcomes. In particular, choices and behaviours can be driven by a fear of failure, which can result in a person ceasing their involvement in a task or project.

It can be hard to regulate how you approach tasks and activities if you have come to see the world in an either/or manner. As a result, it can be hard to see that you almost got there and that such an outcome is actually okay. This is due to a dichotomous way of seeing things — that is, any outcome that is not totally correct or perfect is seen as a failure. This results in a strong focus upon completing tasks and the final outcome, often to the detriment of the process or journey. A/N individuals can therefore miss opportunities to learn how to finetune their behaviours or find value from incremental steps towards an outcome.

It can be helpful to contemplate not being perfect or achieving the perfect outcome. Although this may be scary and unsettling, it can help build resilience. Tolerating thoughts about 'good enough' outcomes can be empowering and help one keep the Harsh Internal Critic down to a dull roar.

The single-minded focus (i.e. on achievement) locks you into one way of seeing the world and therefore you run the risk of repeating well-rehearsed responses — pushing yourself or stopping. Although they are comfortably familiar, there may be newer or different (possibly even more efficient) ways of doing things. Adopting a different perspective can be helpful in realizing that there are options and also second chances. Stepping aside from this one-way of viewing things may just become liberating.

ASPECTS FOR REFLECTION, OPTIONS FOR CHANGE

We can usually identify the positive things that motivate us to participate in an activity, such as a sense of achievement, a change in our social or employment standing, financial gain or a desire to help others. However, are we also aware that sometimes we behave in certain ways specifically to avoid an undesirable outcome? Some things might motivate you to behave in a certain way and therefore move you toward an outcome, while others might drive your behaviour (and you) away from some feared outcome. Potentially, if you can tell the difference between a 'motivator' and a 'driver', you may be able to consciously make a choice about whether to engage in a particular behaviour.

Take a moment to consider the following exercise and note down what is relevant for you in the spheres of your life where you might be operating in an 'all or nothing' manner.

The things I am motivated to achieve at are:

_____

_____

_____

The things I am driven to avoid are:

_____

_____

_____

Dichotomous thinking is where we view the issue/s in front of us in an either/or manner. It means that we see things as being completely one thing or its total opposite — no question, no middle ground and no doubt. The A/N individual is well versed in this way of making sense of the world and it can be one of those driving mechanisms that we have been considering. However, you may not always be aware that this way of viewing the world is operating within you and directing your actions.

So let's play a little word game, one where you try to make links between opposites (that is, where you engage a dichotomous way of viewing the world). Some of these are central to the A/N perspective and way of operating.

Step 1: Over the page are two columns of words in no particular order. See if you can draw lines between each word in the left-hand column and its opposite meaning on the right; for example, black would be connected to white.

black	lazy
perfect	sink
strong	off
focused	cold
float	white
above	useless
an achiever	distracted
industrious	weak
hot	self-indulgent
on	a failure
disciplined	below

Step 2: Review the words you have linked and now draw a circle around the pairs that may be related to the A/N way of seeing the world.

Step 3: Now take a moment to reflect upon which of these circled pairs of words might characterize your personal approach to life in general or your employment situation. Perhaps use a highlighter to make these stand out more. To make it a little more interesting, show the lists to your partner or best friend and ask them to do the highlighter task on your behalf. It will be interesting to see if they highlight the same ones as you. If they are different, might this be an opportunity to become a bit more aware of how you approach life?

5 The Harsh Internal Critic: an unhelpful passenger

The A/N individual does not want to be that person who 'failed' or underperformed. Such behaviour goes against the grain and highlights all the attributes that do not fit with expectations of the self. Due to this, the person might struggle to get past the behaviours or events that were not up to standard and were an embarrassment (to the self).

There tends to be difficulty in forgiving the self for these (perceived) errors or underperformance. This is often attached to a strong sense of self-criticism, which has already been noted as part of the internal make-up of many A/N people. The tendency to beat oneself up psychologically comes about because the A/N person wants (nay, demands) more from themselves.

WHY DO I BEAT MYSELF UP?

We know that it is hard for most of us to not be affected by comments from someone we trust, respect or rely upon. So, how much more powerful might it be if the message and the voice is a familiar one we have lived with for a long time? Surely, if I am angry with myself or disappointed in myself it must be true, and for good reason? However, it is important to see that a key issue is usually overlooked by the A/N individual: that these messages are not tangible. Indeed, they are thoughts, nothing else. The problem is the degree of emotional involvement with these thoughts as well as the meaning and veracity we attribute to them. If we believe and assume that we are our thoughts and that they are true, then there is no room to manoeuvre — we become what we think, and are then driven by these thoughts.

A word that keeps popping up through this exploration is 'believe', as in what we believe to be true. Unfortunately, the more we connect with our internal comments, the bigger the impact of those thoughts can be as we increasingly come to believe them. When you stop to think about it, language is simply a vehicle to convey ideas — powerful, for sure, but nevertheless these words aren't actually alive. It is the meaning we attach to them and the way we bond with them that can be the main problem for the A/N person. This personal meaning tends to be associated with the 'not-quite-up-to-it' message, one that is well rehearsed and may be very familiar to the readers of this book. The A/N person tends to have a manner of talking harshly, ordering about or rigidly expecting certain standards of themselves. The tone can be clinical, distant and even harsh, without the person necessarily realising it. By remaining in a place where there are strong emotions, it proves difficult to shift away from the negativity and, often, a degree of 'stuckness' ensues along with an associated negative rehashing of events. Part of the difficulty here is that you probably don't fully understand why you are so angry at yourself. Nor do you consider that it is possible to change this. Perhaps the biggest issue for folk in this situation is that they lose all sense of distance and objectivity about this ever-present but unhelpful passenger (i.e. the internal critic). In essence, you become one with the language, thoughts and ideas expressed by this voice.

One way to prove how good you are, is to take on a job that is outside of the norm. So it was for Beth, as seen in the following case study.

CASE STUDY
. . . .

Beth had chosen to work in a manual and very physical outdoor role. This saw her pushing herself daily to be as good as the men, if not better. Despite much positive feedback from her employer and her male co-workers, Beth struggled to feel comfortable with her performance or accept that she was a valued member of the crew. There was always something that she could have done better, plus an ever-present nagging doubt that she was letting everyone down. Her inability to accept a 'poor' performance saw Beth constantly second-guessing herself and berating herself with self-generated phrases such as 'How weak are you?' and 'No one is going to respect you for work of that quality'. These thoughts were constant companions throughout the working day but they did not stop there. Beth reported great difficulty with sleep onset, as she would lie in bed reviewing the day and her performance at work.

As we examined this behaviour, it became clear that she was not being fair to herself, nor was she being realistic with her expectations. Further exploration led to the understanding that, from a very early age, Beth's father had placed high and unrealistic expectations on her with all physical tasks. Additionally, he was not shy about sharing his disappointment at her attempts to do things. Throughout her childhood and into adolescence, Beth was repeatedly told that she would amount to nothing, that she was hopeless and that she embarrassed the family. These were powerful words for a young girl to grow up with and as an adult, they drove her to do more, work harder and prove herself, but also to feel uncomfortable with her efforts. The result was a woman who was achieving but could not believe this and therefore would not ease up on herself.

The main reason people tend to automatically run with these internal comments is because they come from the most trusted source: ourselves. But what if you are not really the person being painted in these negative and unhelpful ways within your own mind? Surely, there is a chance that there is more to you than what is being portrayed in that instant, and in the language contained during that moment. Unfortunately, of course, each of these 'instances' is repeated over time and across a number of experiences, because you carry this Harsh Internal Critic with you wherever you go and whatever you do. Perhaps it is time to pause and try to understand what this self-criticism is all about and why the Harsh Internal Critic continues to come along for the journey? Surely there must have been a function for this criticism in the early phase of its development?

For most A/N people, this self-criticism began in the early environment that promoted and expected high performance. The learning and understanding around what is important and valued (by others) may have been intimately associated with negative feedback when goals were not achieved. On those occasions, any failure may have triggered a sense of personal embarrassment. The internal critic usually comes into being as a way of pushing the self to overcome the poor performance and then (hopefully) go on to achieve as expected. The need to push oneself was bound in with this, as it seemed a way to avoid 'failure' and hopefully experience some positive feedback. There would have been your own context in and around this self-critical behaviour from the start. There would have been a reason for it developing but this understanding may have become lost in the mists of time, or become so embedded in certain environments that the original reason is no longer considered. An exploration of this can lead to a more helpful consideration: perhaps it is okay to be nicer to myself. What if this actually is a potential, and one that might pay big dividends in the medium to long term?

If you think about it, over the years there will have been a lot of energy (emotional, cognitive and physical) expended in keeping this anger and disappointment around so you could put the person at fault (you) in their place. If this is the case, it might now be time to ask whether the original function is still valid, and perhaps it is time to review what has been, up to now, accepted as an obvious and self-evident truth.

THE IMPACT OF SELF-CRITICISM

It is probable that self-criticism has the same internal effect as comments and judgments from other people. These self-generated comments may well trigger feelings of anxiety, anger or embarrassment — as if we were being attacked verbally by another person. Whichever direction this criticism comes from (internally or externally), it has essentially the same impact. The result is that the person focuses their attention inwardly and this leads to an evaluation of behaviour in a manner consistent with the tone of the comments i.e. negatively. This means that we often repeatedly shame ourselves internally through this harsh appraisal. In essence, there is a degree of threat involved here — not necessarily to life and limb but to the sense of self and our personal identity.

Humans have developed powerful brains with the capacity to identify and perceive threat that is present and real but also *potentially* relevant in the future. We are able to think and imagine, which provides us with the ability to conjure future problems and therefore feel angry, frightened or overwhelmed in response to an imagined situation. This same process is also possible in relation to internal threats such as self-criticism. Although this is 'me' talking to and about 'myself', the older parts of the brain just know this is ugly and not nice. The brain therefore begins to respond in the same manner as if an external party, such as your boss, is making the negative comments. Threats are met with responses that can include significant arousal (physiological and emotional) and may set in motion strong behaviours and a readiness to respond to the threat.

Embarrassment and shame

We have seen that the A/N person has a strong focus on achievement and driving the self to attain the goals they have set. To get to a place of high achievement in a chosen career, it is likely that the person has pushed themselves but has possibly also been fearful of failing. Often attached to this driven approach is a degree of internal embarrassment/shame that is experienced as a result of encountering underperformance. But importantly, similar to the previous discussion on threat, we can also experience personal embarrassment from *potential* poor performances.

It can be helpful to realize there are various 'types' of personal embarrassment/shame, and this needs a bit of explanation. Here, these words relate to the negative internal views of oneself and one's performance, but there can also be an externally directed sense of embarrassment. This relates to fearful beliefs around what others might think of us following our performance on a task. It is likely that the long-standing trait of self-criticism makes an individual vulnerable to feeling embarrassment about themselves and their performance. One doesn't necessarily need to 'hate' oneself to feel internalized embarrassment, but if there is an underlying hint of inadequacy this can be triggered, especially if you are operating within a competitive environment such as a bonus system or if promotion is being sought.

Strong emotional states such as personal embarrassment can feel very uncomfortable for most of us, and one way to deal with these is to avoid them if possible. This may involve a denial process or, as seen earlier, avoidance behaviours can work to keep the sense of self intact and safe — that is, you do something to ensure you won't encounter the unwanted feelings. You may find that you unwittingly throw yourself into the preparation process for meetings and projects at work to such an extent that the focus is on the doing rather than the feeling. The stronger the negative experience of emotions, the stronger the drive to avoid encountering or experiencing them may be; so, for example, you work very hard, for long hours. This behavioural response can be put in place via the classic demanding language that some high achievers tend to use and be guided by. Key words and phrases that many A/N individuals will recognize and relate to from their internal dialogue include: 'must', 'should', 'have to', 'got to'. These words have the effect of setting up an imperative situation, one where the listener feels there is no choice or option. Unfortunately, avoidance behaviour will only act as a temporary buffer to the feelings bubbling away beneath the ever-present striving for goals.

It can be helpful for you to understand that the self-criticism and sense of embarrassment has come from somewhere and, perhaps more importantly, that it did a job. If we adopt more of a 'functional' approach to this, it can help each of us to feel okay about targeting the unhelpful self-criticism for what it is: a behaviour, and one that we adopted for a reason at some stage. Embarrassment is a reaction, but for our purposes it can also be seen as a driving force within the A/N individual. It is usually in relation to something we feel uncomfortable about. Perhaps a key issue is how this impacts or expresses itself when you encounter difficulties or 'failure' (as A/N individuals tend to describe it). People who drive themselves to achieve may feel the need to prove to themselves and others that they are capable. If the sense of self is built solely upon achievement, then the individual can become exquisitely sensitive to, and primed for action in relation to, particular threats — in this case, potential failure. This priming may mean that the threshold the person responds to (the point at which they feel threatened) is lowered and therefore the threat is, in effect, experienced as greater than it might actually be. Such a situation can result in the Harsh Internal Critic being triggered more easily and, over time, more frequently. This can then result in increased levels of self-criticism and a heightened sense of inadequacy and, when put alongside the goal of high achievement, this combination can bring about a sense of personal embarrassment due to what is perceived as underperformance.

TURNING DOWN THE VOLUME

Each individual needs to find a way to step back from these negative ideas, thoughts and internal comments. By doing this, you can better develop a degree of objectivity, which can help keep you safe from the potentially harmful and destabilizing effects of these internal comments. To lessen or take away the negative effects of this self-criticism, the person needs to be able to replace this unhelpful dialogue with something more beneficial, or at least less undermining.

The fact that strong emotions are involved will mean that it is not as simple as 'telling myself' that things will be better and there isn't really a problem. Even if some awareness is developed, it might not be easy to bring about change by just saying, 'I won't do this again.' The self-blaming needs to be replaced with something else, something that accommodates the heightened (and raw) emotions such as personal embarrassment. Tolerating the distress and concern around feeling inadequate (remember:

this may well be a biased perception and not a reality) is also an important aspect. It will be more helpful in the long run if you can move on from avoidance of these feelings to being able to work with the internal dialogue plus start to be somewhat kinder to yourself. If you can see the negativity within a context, then you can start to see that there is some choice about whether you treat yourself in such a manner.

As with all things in life, there is usually a reason for our behaviour; it serves some sort of purpose. For the A/N person, this behaviour is often associated with fear of failure, such as not living up to their own exacting standards. By focusing solely upon the task and outcome, you unfortunately tend to overlook the process and don't take note of how important your efforts and experiences are. A/N individuals expect a lot of themselves and tend not to give credit for the effort put in — they only see that they have fallen short of the mark. Nor have they learnt to value effort for its own sake. You may overlook the fact that there is a process, or journey, involved and that this may be as important as the outcome.

Interestingly, when a therapist introduces the idea of learning to cut themselves some slack, there is often a recoil in horror from the A/N individual and an immediate sense that such an approach would not be appropriate or even possible. Sitting behind this is a long learning history of seeing anything other than full-on effort as being slack, self-indulgent or perhaps the biggest insult of all: lazy. It can be quite sad to witness this struggle to care for themselves or see the merit in judging themselves by the kinder standards they might apply to others. When you ask an A/N person how they relate to other folk who struggle, they can invariably come up with appropriate explanations and reasons for why those people may not have met their own goals. They demonstrate an ability to account for context and the intangible factors that can impact performance — but usually only for others. However, if you can relate to this, you probably also find it very difficult to account for such variables and how they relate to yourself. As if different rules within the universe apply to you! This is so unfair, as it means mistakes are constantly replayed and the resulting sense of anger, personal embarrassment and heartache colours the A/N person's ability to feel good about themselves.

This constant self-judging has become an art form for most A/N people. Although it may have started long ago and for possibly understandable reasons, this function has now become lost in the passage of time. A/N individuals seem to hold onto an awareness that initially they learnt to shape their performance around how to do things 'correctly'. Similarly, they can often see that this learning was around getting better and then maintaining the new high(er) standards. However, over time, it has gone beyond this positive guidance phase and become more like the classic Sergeant Major who yells, demands and harasses to get immediate and uniform responses. It is important to acknowledge that A/N people are not continuously engaged in an internal battle where they scream at themselves inside their own heads day and night. Rather, this self-bullying (for that is what it really has become) tends to be triggered when they encounter challenges and poor performance. The default option is to see such behaviour in relation to the outcome, not notice the effort or indeed be self-supportive. It is also important to note that this behaviour doesn't necessarily signal a strong sense of hatred towards the self. The majority of A/N people I have met are not caught up in an overwhelming sense of uselessness or personal dislike. Rather, they have come to believe this criticism is part of learning to meet goals and excel; interesting indeed, that they have chosen a benign and helpful interpretation of such a negative behaviour. Unfortunately, this criticism has got out of control and become so automatic that they may not recognize when they are doing it, let alone to what extent. Given that A/N people basically like themselves and are comfortable spending time with themselves, it should be possible to help them learn to disengage from this unhelpful approach.

Learning to disengage

You will be pleased to hear that the goal of shifting this behaviour is not to turn yourself into an 'average' or 'lazy' person. Rather, it is about helping you to apply the same realistic standards that you may apply to others! A key factor is helping you to be able to disengage from the Harsh Internal Critic at important times, such as when you are starting to struggle or are encountering a setback. It is about helping you to also see that this negative self-talk taps into strong emotions; it is not just about words inside the head. These words relate to, trigger and may also enhance emotions. The words and emotions are also related to memories and contexts. This is how the brain operates; it likes to group things together as this is an efficient sorting and retrieval system. I often tell clients that the 'flavour' of a thought is transmitted and opens up other parts of the network, but generally only those aspects with the same 'flavour'. So, if our responses to a challenge or setback are negative and self-deprecatory, then the thoughts and emotions around this are more likely to be unhelpful as well. These will access the memory banks and open up folders of similar unsuccessful encounters or outcomes. Obviously, this is less than helpful if one is trying to work through a difficult situation and all they can recall are previous 'failures'.

It is important to realise that you can't eliminate these emotions by throwing yourself into more of the behaviour, such as pushing on with the task no matter what. Being angry at the self will not bring about the goal of being perfect; the latter is not actually possible, anyway. Flexibility needs to be tapped into, so that the standards applied are beneficial and realistic. (No, that does not mean second-rate!) Simply beating yourself up psychologically does not solve anything.

It can also be helpful to learn to pull back and get some perspective, to see if you are applying (to yourself) the same rules you apply to the rest of the world. The sense of personal embarrassment mentioned earlier is triggered because the A/N person does not want to see themselves as that person who has 'failed'. What if this 'black and white' application of rules and judgment could be shifted so that you realize you might not have failed, therefore you do not need to feel this sense of embarrassment?

In essence, the self-critical judging has brought about a conflict with the primary value of being on top of things. It can be really helpful to learn that a better approach is to adjust expectations, rather than simply starting to be 'nice' to yourself, which can bring up images of self-indulgence. It is really about being brave enough to look at things differently and not to just go with the well-rehearsed comments from long ago. Adjusting expectations is *not* about giving up on standards. If anything, it is a refinement of a balance between achievement and sustainability. From such a perspective, a more solid sense of self may begin to emerge, one that can cope with achievements, challenges *and* disappointments. Now, doesn't that sound like a better recipe for (sustainable) success?

IN SUMMARY

There is a voice that you know well and it is not always a comforting or even supportive one. This familiarity makes it hard to ignore and also gives the statements an air of authenticity — or is that authority? As a result, you have probably come to accept the comments as appropriate and 'true'. However, you are hopefully now beginning to realize that this Harsh Internal Critic is not really concerned with motivating you or even helping you to up your game and be more successful. Rather, it is a long-standing expression of the negativity and fear related to performance and achievement. The language employed is more about pointing out your perceived shortcomings than offering active problem-solving approaches. Why this voice is hard to ignore is simple: it is your own!

Messages that have been given to us by important others are powerful and, if they are said often enough, we take them on board. This results in us using them as guidelines, and they help shape our expectations of ourselves. What we tend to forget is that these messages were from a particular context but they now have a life of their own and seem to relate to *all* aspects of our lives. Perhaps it is time to pause and ask whether the original context is still relevant or indeed valid any more? Maybe by doing this you can start to explore other ways of making sense of your performance and identify new ways that not only help you solve problems but also motivate you.

Because this unhelpful passenger so eagerly points out where we go wrong, we seem to either be constantly near a crisis of confidence or repeatedly confronted with our perceived inabilities. This has implications for how we see ourselves and can result in a sense of personal embarrassment. This is a problem, as we may then struggle to let go of the 'failures', run the risk of being overwhelmed by strong negative emotions and may also find it difficult to ask for help. This chews up a lot of emotional energy and can get us stuck in a rut, whereby it is hard to generate any positivity about ourselves or our potential.

There is room in our lives for appropriate, objective and realistic self-appraisal, as these things can help us finetune our performance, adjust and adapt. However, the Harsh Internal Critic is neither objective nor is s/he realistic much of the time. As a result, you may be unfairly judging your performance and becoming acutely aware of what you are doing wrong — and not noticing what you are doing right. It is only fair that you offer yourself the chance to see if you are being realistic and, if not, it might be time to dampen the authority that seems to come along with this critical voice.

ASPECTS FOR REFLECTION, OPTIONS FOR CHANGE

No, having a voice inside your head telling you how bad you are doing is not a sign of madness. This familiar voice — which excels in pointing out your mistakes — isn't an alien intruder. It is a looped recording of long-standing messages about perfect performance and pushing yourself, that is expressed in your own 'speak'. It represents the lessons given to you by others long ago, about always being the best.

A key approach to dealing with this unwanted and unhelpful passenger is to find ways to dampen the volume, decrease the impact and lessen the hold the messages have upon you; it is not to spend endless energy hating it. In fact, what would be really beneficial is if you can reframe the familiar role of this voice from that of a 'Harsh Internal Critic' to one of a 'Quality Control Advisor'. This makes it possible to hear the messages from a different perspective and see the 'feedback' (*not criticism*) as an opportunity to monitor your progress and adjust as needed.

A helpful approach is to learn to refocus your perspective from the critical approach to a more positive one that affirms you. The challenge is to gain a more balanced view of events and adopt a more supportive stance with yourself. Within this, try to identify what your strengths and skills are, rather than just seeing that things have come unstuck. Remind yourself of previous times when you have been able to fix things up, use appropriate strategies or problem-solve issues, as these may well reflect a more accurate image of your ability. By tapping into previous achievements and good outcomes, you will disengage from the parts of your brain associated with responding to threat. Those areas are the ones that kick your nervous system into overdrive and ready you for any threats. Unfortunately, if you are in a negative or defeatist frame of mind, this will only key you into your perceived failures more and more. Conversely, if you can generate a more positive and accepting stance to your situation, you have a better chance of activating those parts of the brain related to feeling good and in control. Surely this is a better place to be exploring problem-solving options from?

If you have got this far through the book, it is time to consider not slavishly following the unhelpful thoughts and expectations you at times have about yourself and your abilities. For example, when confronted with a difficult situation do you see the world from a black-and-white perspective that may trap you into inescapable and potentially unfair conclusions about your abilities? If you challenge those critical messages, you may be able to avoid the self-defeating behaviours that often come racing in next.

An effective way to begin doing this is to notice what happens when you encounter a difficult situation. You may notice that you immediately have thoughts telling you how useless you are or that the task is beyond you. Up until now, these automatic and negative thoughts may have been accepted as being gospel. But what is the actual evidence for these statements? How true are they and is there another perspective? Simple questioning like this fits with the way the brain operates and is also much better than just yelling at yourself! The brain is a logical machine that likes to answer questions and if you set it a question, you engage the logic circuitry rather than the negative, self-bashing emotional mechanisms. Such questions also allow you to see if the harsh statements are actually true. If they don't stand up to logical scrutiny, you may be able to replace these unhelpful thoughts and comments with more useful alternatives.

Try this

Have a piece of paper and a pen handy. Recall a recent time when a task you undertook wasn't going too well. Once you get a clear memory or image of the event, try to focus in on the thoughts that came into your mind about things not working out. They may have been something like: 'Here we go again, another stuff up' or 'Useless sod, you can't get anything right' or even 'This is hopeless, what's the point?'. Of course there are many variations on this theme but for a lot of A/N people, the automatic thoughts they have in response to difficulties are self-blaming and negative. Now write down a very brief description of the situation and then beside this what the immediate thoughts were. Now repeat this same process three more times with different situations; note that the situations you choose don't have to be major catastrophes.

Do you notice anything about the type of thoughts and words that were running through your head at these challenging times? Did they set you up to feel good about yourself and help with problem solving or . . . ?

Now for each thought you have written down, ask yourself at least two of the following simple questions:

- What is the actual evidence for these statements?
- How true are these comments or beliefs?
- Is there another perspective I could take?

What does the logical, non-emotional part of your brain offer as answers to these new questions? Might the answers set you on a different course than the previously accepted negative comments? If so, perhaps you could give this simple technique a go — challenging your thoughts with the above questions — next time you encounter a challenging situation.

Try this

Another useful technique to deal with the Harsh Internal Critic and his/her comments is to shift to an external or different perspective. An effective way to do this is to ask yourself what a valued and trusted friend, colleague or mentor might say in response to the situation you are encountering. This requires a bit of pre-planning but, once sorted, it can be a powerful way to help yourself disengage from the internal bashing you are receiving or are about to receive. In order to use this technique, you need to think of someone you know well and whose opinion you trust implicitly. Try to choose a person who has qualities that are opposite to the harsh and demeaning approach of the internal critic. Think of someone who is level headed, able to sort out reality from a fearful appraisal and perhaps is also able to generate options for managing difficult situations. These are the type of attributes you could benefit from encountering in place of the current unhelpful and self-deprecating statements. It is hard to simply 'replace' longstanding ways of seeing the world, so this technique helps you try new ones on for size and become familiar with them.

Let's now put this approach into practice. Recall a situation where things were going wrong and you were being critical of yourself. Settle back in a quiet, comfortable environment and try to recall the putdowns that were offered up to yourself about this event. Not nice, were they?! What is the effect on you of hearing these words and interpretations of the events?

Now, see if you can visualize the person whose opinion or perspective you trust and try to hear their voice. The aim is to hear what this person might say about the difficulties encountered or the mistakes made. If you know this person well, you will have a fair idea of what they will say, plus how they will interpret the situation and outcomes. Allow yourself to listen to this person and consider their take on the situation. How is it different to what you were saying to yourself, and what is the effect of hearing this different perspective? Remember, this new 'voice' or perspective is from someone you trust and therefore it is worthwhile acknowledging that their take may well be valid and one that you could consider adopting.

Practise the above approach by reviewing past situations — first from your own perspective and then from that of the trusted advisor. If you can make the image of this person as real as possible and hear their voice, you will be better able to relate to their message. When you are next in a challenging situation and you notice that you are starting to dump on yourself, pause, take a few calming breaths and then ask yourself: What would (make sure you name him/her) say about this or about my performance? Hopefully this will allow you to consider an alternative perspective and, after a while, you might find that you don't automatically criticize yourself and your efforts.

6 Striving for perfection, or needing to be perfect?

One of the things I have noticed from clinical experience is that perfectionism often goes hand in hand with the A/N personality-style. In this chapter, we will consider the strong attention to detail and pushing of oneself to obtain a flawless outcome that many A/N people operate by. They regularly strive to do their best and tend to be bitterly disappointed if the result is not top notch.

Within the individual, there can be a powerful drive which sees them sometimes become overly focused on a task until they reach a (very) high self-set level of accomplishment. As noted earlier, the fear of not producing a perfect performance can lead to a type of cognitive paralysis or procrastination, where the A/N individual may not be willing to start a project due to a sense that it will not be up to the level they require. This chapter will explore how the perfectionistic tendencies fit in with, or even promote, the A/N approach to life.

As the title of this chapter suggests, there are certain traits which can have an important influence on how we approach things. Of particular relevance here is the issue of perfectionistic traits. It is not being suggested that these are fully formed at birth, nor do they appear complete at a particular birthday or milestone. Rather, these traits are developed over time and can also be shaped by forces external to the individual. Within all of us, there may be more or less of a natural tendency towards a focus on things being 'right'. (For our purposes, though, we are not considering clinical conditions such as Obsessive Compulsive Disorder or Autistic Spectrum Disorders, both of which can have a strong focus on orderliness, correctness and specificity.) However, some people exhibit strong traits that promote a need to have things completed but with the emphasis upon correctness and high quality. Therefore, to make more sense of this style of interacting with the world, it can be helpful to gain a grasp of factors relevant to perfection. Perhaps by understanding this a bit better, we can see that perfectionism is not (as our subject group would see it) a matter of being completely present or not; neither is it entirely useful or entirely problematic. It may actually be that one can have a leaning towards high standards and doing a great job but also have some flexibility to tolerate the occasional not-so-great performance. If we can view perfectionistic traits (and expressions of these) as being on a continuum, then we may not need to eliminate the desire to do well. Rather, bringing about understanding of this internal pressure more fully, and learning to identify when it is starting to impact events, can be beneficial. This can allow its effect to be varied, to bring about a more helpful outcome.

TRUE CONFESSION TIME

As a group, clinical psychologists tend to skew towards being perfectionists. The question is whether the training makes one like this or whether people like this are attracted to the profession. I think it is the latter. We tend to find it difficult to write short reports as we might leave something 'important' out. Additionally, we tend to have angst over the right words to ensure the accuracy of what we are trying to say.

I have to put my hand up to say that I have leant towards perfectionistic tendencies for many years. My excuse is that I was born a Virgo, a star sign that inherently describes perfection and fussiness (now there's an example of one of those rationalizations we mentioned earlier!). My wife has been raising an eyebrow for many a year at my perseverance with tasks beyond what is actually necessary. A good example of this is within my chosen hobby of restoring old Japanese motorcycles. One might say this has become an outlet for my perfectionistic tendencies, as I have endeavoured to restore my bikes to the exact specifications they had when they left the factory in Japan over 40 years ago. In the spirit of openness, I shall share an example that illustrates my sameness-as-you and also underlines the problems (and sometimes pointlessness) of perfectionistic tendencies.

I needed to replace the brake linings on my 1971 Kawasaki 500 and immediately set out on an international quest to find original brake shoes with the factory-original linings for the bike. This was due to my belief that for the bike to be correct, it had to be 100 per cent correct — that is, all parts had to be the same as the day it left Japan. I eventually found a set on eBay and entered a bidding war with some gentleman who obviously thought the same as me. The cost went up and up (in US dollars) but I was determined to win and eventually did so. The price of postage was not insignificant either, *but* I did have the original shoes and linings, which of course meant my restoration was going to be 'correct'.

After fitting the new shoes and test-riding the bike, I was disappointed with the braking performance and also frustrated that my efforts were no advance on the problem I was addressing. I expressed this to a fellow rider who has much more mechanical nous than myself, and he brusquely stated, 'What the heck did you expect?' and then added, 'You bought a 45-year-old product which is made of obsolete and inefficient material and expected it to perform well in the 21st century.' After more discussion, he went on to add that I could have taken the old shoes into a local brake centre and had the linings redone with a modern compound that would have been much more effective and cost me a fraction of what I paid. He also pointed out the (now) blindingly obvious fact that no one can actually see what material the linings are made of as they are hidden inside the wheel!

Hmmm, food for thought . . . and personal reflection, perhaps. What this episode taught me was that the quest to obtain perfection can lead to a single-minded following of a pathway even though there might be more realistic, practical (and cheaper) options that could achieve the same or better outcome. By obtaining an outside perspective, I was now able to see that I could attain the goals I had set myself plus enjoy the outcomes for what they were, rather than what I felt they should have been. In reality, even with modern brake linings the bike looks original!

. . . .

There currently isn't a complete or universally agreed-upon definition of perfectionism. However, there is some acceptance that it may consist of a number of aspects. This can include it being a characteristic of personality but also that it involves some aspects of cognition (thoughts and processing) plus behaviour. There does also seem to be some agreement amongst researchers and therapists that it involves the setting of high standards and may, for some, be accompanied by self-criticism when personal standards are not met.

However, striving to be the best you possibly can be is not necessarily a bad thing, and it is a well-evidenced truth that setting high standards can have a lot of positive spin-offs. Where would the Olympic Games be if standards were not set at a high level? They would, in effect, be a pretty mediocre track meet with any country bumpkin able to turn up and throw a spear about. Instead, we see the positive pursuit of high standards, celebration of success and the many positive aspects of a global activity. As we will hopefully come to see, having high goals and standards is not the problem, nor does it have to be a major character flaw.

PROBLEMS ACCOMPANYING THE QUEST FOR PERFECTION

If we are to better understand perfectionism and therefore the impact on the A/N individual, we need to realize that it is about much more than just the setting of high standards. There can also be concern about mistakes or poor performance and some doubt about personal potential, both of which sit alongside these self-set standards. Additionally, some perfectionists struggle with the ability to congratulate themselves and be comfortable with any level of achievement. It is suggested here that all of these aspects are to some degree present in and relevant to the A/N person.

The A/N person tends to judge their performance at any given point not only by high standards but also the critical self-evaluation discussed in the previous chapter. If performance can be evaluated without slipping into this negative self-judgment, it can be possible to modulate one of the unhealthy drivers that maintains the singular focus upon outcomes. It may well be that the negative self-evaluation is acting as a pathway away from positive goal-setting and leading instead to the less helpful driving of oneself to get the perfect outcome. Thus, to make better sense of what drives you as an A/N person and to better understand the impact of your behaviours, it can be useful to bear in mind this negative, regularly running commentary. This unhelpful passenger may be one of the important aspects of what turns perfectionism from the positive and useful to the maladaptive.

The high standards of a perfectionist can also be directed towards other people, where the perfectionist comes to expect or demand that others perform to a similarly high standard. However, this can be patently unfair at times. The other person may have no idea they are being judged or held to account, which can make it bewildering (and frustrating) that they are thought of as 'not up to it' by the person evaluating them. This of course is a potential recipe for disaster and strife in both personal and professional situations. The perfectionist, at times, can become so disenchanted by others (who don't even know they are under scrutiny) that they begin to express their frustration. For the A/N person, this may result in a sense of frustration to the point where they consider it impossible to 'trust' others to do the right thing. One outcome is that they do not delegate tasks, plus they may have a sense of disappointment and disillusionment about those they work with. This can then lead to the perfectionist adding to their own workload — with an imbalance in the dynamics and operating levels with co-workers or employees. Obviously, this adds to the burden of tasks and can see the A/N person push themselves to do even more, in the mistaken belief that others are not up to the task and the only person they can rely on is . . . themselves. Over time, this builds up the workload and increases the risk of burn-out.

A final twist in this tale is that perfectionists often believe the high levels of achievement they exhibit are demanded and expected of them by others. They see this as an inescapable trap, as they are convinced others are holding them to very high standards. Unfortunately, the A/N person seldom pauses to check out whether, indeed, these expectations are true. If you talk to workers who operate like this (particularly if they are returning from a workplace injury) they will often push beyond their tolerance levels as they respond to a combination of their own internal demands and the perceived expectations from, for example, their employer or manager. Interestingly, when you encourage the A/N person to actually ask the employer about their performance and to establish what the expectations are, there is often clear feedback that the boss is happy with the output — that is, much of the pressure and performance concerns tend to be self-generated.

As stated earlier, having high standards is not necessarily all bad. However, when these standards are aligned with an A/N style of thinking, the result can be a merciless striving for unrealistic goals, with internal chastising that acts as a negative energizer. I recall a client whose passion was pigeon breeding and racing. He identified potential benefits from having the best possible environment for his birds to live in. As a result, he set about building them a new aviary. This was going to be the Taj Mahal of aviaries and something that would also bring him kudos amongst fellow fanciers. However, it never quite got finished as there were always adjustments and modifications that 'needed' to be done. When I reflected that he had been working on this project for nigh on seven years (!) he offered multiple reasons why things weren't up to the required standard. The question then became who was he doing this for and whose standards was he trying to meet. As far as I could tell (and I readily admit to being no expert on pigeons), his birds had been eating, preening, sleeping, doing the stuff that pigeons do and happily making baby pigeons within the old, apparently unsatisfactory, housing over this entire seven-year period. In contrast, the breeder was a frustrated and unhappy man who could only see that things were 'not quite right yet'.

When goals slip from one's grasp, the self-criticism becomes stronger and the individual can experience a double whammy of personal embarrassment and guilt related to the perceived 'failure'. This is a sense of shame that s/he has not lived up to their own standards and those that they believe others are holding them to. The guilt is around having let themselves down, plus the concern that they have shown the world they were not up to the task. So there may well be nothing wrong with aiming for high levels of achievement *but* what if the individual builds their sense of self around this issue, such that it rests solely upon the striving and attainment? Such a situation has the potential to turn things towards the negative and problematic. Once again, the issue for those with a tendency to take an A/N approach is that if you start to see yourself as being capable or worthwhile only when you achieve highly, you cannot consider yourself capable or worthwhile if you do a less-than-perfect job. The problem for A/N folk is that they tend to apply their high standards to everything they attempt in the important areas of their life, then judge themselves solely by outcomes rather than effort. Unfortunately, if one area is perceived as deficient, this can be enough to wipe away all other achievements no matter how many other projects were actually successful. In essence, you may end up discounting your successes and placing an emphasis upon your failures. This, over time, opens the door for a level of negative self-judgment that can have implications for mood levels and personal confidence.

THE GOOD, THE BAD AND THE UGLY (OUTCOMES)

Recent understanding of perfection shows it to be both complex and multilevel. Research suggests there can be both positive and negative dimensions of perfection, as discussed earlier. Additionally, it is clear that some individuals can live with and manage this drive for top performance and excellent outcomes. Ellam-Dyson and Palmer (2010) refer to 'healthy perfectionists' who are able to focus on and work towards a desired goal but do not have the tendency to give themselves a hard time if they do not meet their aims. These 'healthy perfectionists' therefore do not seem to embody a key and ever-present (negative) element of the A/N personality — the Harsh Internal Critic.

This raises an interesting point: if A/N folk have strong perfectionistic traits and also the internal critic, might it be possible to bring about a more positive approach by helping the individual learn to manage that critic, to develop a 'healthy' approach to perfectionism? Such an approach may help retain a more manageable, yet still positive, focus and begin to dial down the tendency to push too far and hard. This may help bring about a change in how workplace tasks are approached without altering the essence of the individual (i.e. someone who wishes to do well in their career). What if you could keep valued aspects of yourself, such as being achievement-focused, while modulating the level of effort on tasks, and therefore reduce personal levels of angst and stress? For perfectionists operating at Ellam-Dyson and Palmer's 'unhealthy' end of the spectrum, the stress is prolonged and is a bit like driving your car with one foot on the brake while pressing the accelerator harder and harder, all the while expecting more performance. In the short term, little happens to the car except higher levels of unpleasant noise but if this inappropriate driving style continues, parts of the motor will begin to be affected. Within the individual, this can mean physical, cognitive or emotional wear and tear!

Within clinical work and the associated literature, it has long been noted that aspects associated with having high standards can be risky. In recent times, more and more research is reinforcing this point and we now think that perfectionism has a role to play in the beginning and maintenance of a number of clinical problems. Some examples of these are anxiety-based conditions, mood problems and eating disorders. The type of perfectionism relevant here is the intrapersonal one, whereby high expectations are placed upon oneself to achieve goals that may be unrealistic or unsustainable. Unfortunately, there often is no self-limiting or adjusting mechanism inherent in this process. Thus, once you reach the goal, you immediately reset the target — but always in an upward direction. This is due to the fact the person feels the initial level must have been too easy if they were able to meet it! It therefore becomes increasingly harder to meet the self-set goals and the person finds themselves on a 'mission impossible'. As a result, such individuals may be vulnerable to anxiety and/or depression.

Anxiety, depression and perfectionism entwined

One reason for the potential onset of anxiety and depression in such circumstances is that both these conditions share a mechanism that helps maintain their existence: perfection drivers. If the A/N person engages with the world via a strongly operating perfection driver, s/he may be at higher risk of mood-related problems should things not go according to plan. Therefore, it can be useful to understand that the perfectionistic approach to life may be a legitimate target if the aim is to bring about meaningful change. For those who have suffered burn-out, focusing solely on either mood or anxiety may be akin to only smoothing the upper edges on the proverbial iceberg — there is much more lurking below the surface which can continue to create problems. However, if the perfectionistic tendencies can be modulated, then gains may be achieved with the A/N style of behaviour *plus* any mood and anxiety issues that are impacting the individual.

. . . .

You will have noticed by now that this book is not about eliminating or 'curing' problems. Rather, it presents an approach of understanding what factors are operating within the individual at a given time and then considers how to modulate these. To this end, empowering yourself with knowledge and skills about all aspects of the drive to be perfect will have a more lasting impact than just being told to lower your standards a bit. Remember that old adage about teaching a person how to fish rather than just giving them a fish? It is a waste of therapeutic energy to simply suggest to you, the A/N person, that your high standards need to be eliminated. This is threatening, since, as you know full well, such a perspective has helped you achieve highly. If it is suggested that you simply let go of this approach, an A/N person will feel vulnerable and the tendency to dichotomous thinking will immediately take them to a place of fear that they will become a slob with no standards . . . and therefore no potential!

There is a wealth of well-established therapeutic approaches with techniques to help you gain a sense of mastery over the perfection driver you may have been living with. Two of these approaches are Cognitive Behavioural Therapy (CBT) and Acceptance and Commitment Therapy (ACT). Both of these therapies have an understanding that, in some way or other, cognitions (thoughts, appraisals and decisions) plus their resulting behaviours can not only create problems but also keep alive the difficulties. The approach put forward by this book is to help you learn what 'driver' is being triggered and when the unhelpful thoughts, feelings and comments are coming into play so that you can manage or modulate the symptoms.

To make a lasting change (in behaviour), it may not be useful to focus on altering the high standards in isolation. Rather, it may prove to be of more benefit to learn how to manage the self-critical voice that comments upon and drives certain unhelpful behaviours. So if you are setting career goals, don't think you have to aim low; that perfectionistic streak may serve you well as you undertake projects within the workplace, as it has the potential to help you achieve highly and demonstrate your abilities. The key is to ensure that you are motivated by positive reinforcement and the pursuit of excellence, as opposed to being driven by a fear of failure. The latter is more likely to result in you focusing on possible errors and putting in longer hours, with potentially less efficiency plus reduced job satisfaction. The former should result in you setting clearer goals and, if it is complemented by a high sense of self-efficacy, you may be able to confidently choose and move in a beneficial direction.

IN SUMMARY

Perfectionistic traits are not evil or wrong. However, they can sometimes take on a life of their own and become unhelpful.

Indeed, they can become a trap that is hard to escape from, one where we begin to expect ourselves to be perfect. Ask yourself, in the cold light of day, whether perfection is actually a realistic or attainable goal. If it isn't, you may be setting yourself up for some heavy-duty heartache whereby you constantly feel that you are failing, only to then readjust your goals. Unfortunately, this tends to be upwards, rather than towards a realistic level. These perfectionistic traits are not, in and of themselves, a problem. Rather, it is how much of these you operate with and what you do with them that counts.

If you strive to improve, you can go places that were previously inaccessible. Think about top athletes and their constant quest to run faster, throw further or jump higher. These high achievers readjust and realign their goals and technique to the nth degree but they realize that subtle changes can pay big dividends. Unfortunately, if the quest for better performance is accompanied by harsh judgment and negative criticism then things can come unstuck quite quickly. This is particularly so during times of stress, pressure and demand — when one needs to perform at their peak.

There can be a 'healthy' perfection driver, where we challenge ourselves to extend our performance and try to go further in a desired direction for positive reasons. There is also the less positive perfection driver, where we dump on ourselves immediately and continuously when we do not meet the targets we set for ourselves. Unfortunately, A/N people tend to operate in the realm of the latter. As a result, when you encounter situations where you do not meet the self-set high goals, you tend to be confronted by a disparaging appraisal of performance (sadly, your own). This way of approaching life comes with risks, such as lowered confidence, burn-out, anxiety and depression.

You might find that your goals are being shaped by unhelpful and perhaps misperceived information. This is usually self-generated, but it can leak out so that you start to second-guess the expectations of others and whether they are judging you. Many A/N people drive themselves to meet targets or levels of operating that they believe are being set by external people and agencies. Unfortunately, the A/N individual does not always take time to check in with these significant others to see if the expectations and standards are as they believe. If they aren't, the A/N person may be pushing themselves needlessly and bringing about unnecessary pressures and problems. While there are some workplaces where the external standards are even higher than one's own, the point here is to check things out first rather than drive yourself to distraction based on assumptions.

All things in moderation is a good maxim. This applies to the goals and expectations you set yourself. With ever increasing standards comes a potentially disproportionate cost in terms of physical, cognitive and emotional energy. The extra effort put in to get an 'A+' on an exam is usually well beyond the actual, measureable difference between an 'A' and an 'A+'. This is not to suggest you shouldn't try to extend yourself or do better. You should, however, weigh things up within a personal and functional context and then make a conscious decision on the effort to be expended in relation to the value of the goal you are setting. This is instead of automatically driving yourself to achieve at a higher level without understanding what is behind such decisions. Don't throw away your desire to achieve or your personal expectation about making gains. Instead, try to understand what is driving you at any point and check in to see if the goals are realistic, attainable and appropriate.

ASPECTS FOR REFLECTION, OPTIONS FOR CHANGE

Language can trap us. Perhaps it is time to give some thought to how you verbally prepare for tasks and, more importantly, how you talk to yourself if things don't turn out perfectly. If, before you start a task, you regularly find yourself using phrases like 'I must …', 'I have to…' or 'This needs to be …', then you could be following that perfection driver. Try replacing those demanding words and phrases with ones that give you a chance of succeeding, such as 'A realistic timeframe for this would be…' or 'The options for this are …'.

If, after the task is done, you find yourself using unhelpful, derogatory and judgmental phrases, you are probably stuck in that unpleasant space that is ruled by the Harsh Internal Critic. Instead, try focusing on what you did achieve rather than what you didn't. If you are starting to judge your performance harshly, refer back to p. 104 and the discussion of a trusted person, then ask yourself: 'What would [name of your trusted person] say about my performance today?' This way you are not generalizing about all performances and letting that automatic negative thinking kick into gear.

Try this

Your perfection driver is probably embedded deeply in schemas that were laid down long ago. In order to lessen the impact, you may need a step-by-step strategy to 'de-automate' the process. *Before* you start a task or project, follow the steps below.

1. Ask yourself, 'What is my goal today, with this task, here, in front of me now?'
2. Reflect on your honest answer then ask yourself, 'Is it reasonable and fair to expect the performance, outcome or timeframe that I have just set myself?'
3. If the answer is no, then go back to Step 1 and recalibrate your answer to account for the realities of this situation *here and now* (not what your perfection driver is saying).
4. Move on to Step 2 again and ask yourself the same question. If the answer is still no, go back to Step 1 again. Repeat this process as often as it takes for you to shift from the need for perfection to a place of realistic goal-setting.
5. Once the answer at Step 2 is yes, then go ahead and do the task — but work to the realistic guidelines you have set.

Few things in life come without a cost. Striving to meet high standards can lead to great things but it can extract quite a price if we 'fail' to meet the goal. Consider the following.

- Have you ever taken the time to reflect upon your reactions and internal dialogue when you do not meet your goals?
- What happens to your emotions in situations where you come face to face with your 'imperfection' (as you might term it)?
- Do you allow yourself to enjoy or savour your achievements when you do succeed, or do you simply reset your standards even higher?

One of the things noted earlier was that the desire for a perfect outcome can lead to both procrastination and paralysis. So, just to balance things out a little: it appears that procrastination may not always be a recipe for disaster. It is rumoured that Mozart wrote the overture to *Don Giovanni* on the morning that the opera premiered . . . and by all accounts that turned out all right!

7 Health and wellbeing

Throughout the book so far, we have acknowledged that the A/N personality-style can have significant benefits for the individual in terms of financial reward, status acquired, promotions gained and useful connections made, as well as a personal sense of achievement and an enhanced sense of self. However, there is seldom anything that is totally pure and positive. Most of the time there are costs attached to or associated with anything that is rewarding. You make money on investments but you pay more tax; you develop a taste for a sweet dessert but your waistline increases!

Similarly, there tend to be costs associated with the A/N approach to activity and life in general. However, these costs are not always easily identified. This can be a trap for the A/N individual because, as you will recall, one of the main attributes is the tendency to focus on the proximal and potentially positive outcomes. Seldom is much thought given to the delayed, negative outcomes (unless, of course, we tap into the fear of failure). By seeing the connection between hard work, long hours and personal talents, you regularly reinforce the behaviours that bring this about. As a result, you may continue on the road to success and tend not to notice the warning signs along the journey. These negative outcomes can, either singly or in combination, become a threat to the individual, their emotional and physical wellbeing, employment situation or family relationships. In this chapter we shall therefore look at some of the potential challenges that can result from following the A/N approach to life. Hopefully by being forewarned, you can be forearmed.

PHYSICAL HEALTH

Being healthy is a complex and multifaceted issue. It is not just about the status of one's muscles and bones and it does not depend solely on physical wellbeing.

One of the key factors often overlooked by individuals and the medical world at large is the role of personality structure and its effect on choices and behaviours. The A/N personality-style can have both direct and indirect influences on how we view and relate to health and also how we interact with the medical world. This approach sets up a range of expectations, beliefs and responses that may be regularly reinforced through life.

The learning experiences that result in an A/N personality-style tend to promote stoicism and self-reliance. Therefore, if a doctor is consulted, it may be quite late in the piece due to the conflicting demands of work and other responsibilities. This can have implications for illness progression as well as treatment options and outcomes. Once treatment has begun, there may also be a number of challenges for the A/N individual in following treatment protocols, ranging from taking medications through to attending medical appointments.

It has already been suggested that the learning experiences within family, school and work environments shape the perspectives of the A/N individual as s/he grows up. The family of origin may have, either subtly or clearly, demonstrated certain behaviours around health as well and this perhaps was reflected in parental responses to reports of feeling unwell and minor injury as the child developed. If the family valued performance and getting on with things, there may have been a high threshold to be met before outside assistance was sought. This is not to suggest that parents of A/N individuals were neglectful or dismissive of important health issues. Rather, part of the valued attribute of 'being in control' and coping may have been the ability to tolerate minor ailments and illnesses. Additionally, time off work may not have been something that was modelled in the family and therefore days off school may have been few and far between. This would be a reflection of parental expectations that one should get on and perform their duty or role, and only take time off in circumstances that 'really' require it. (I have more than one medical colleague who has sent a child to school with 'a sore arm', only to find out later that it was actually fractured!)

In some sense, we are talking about a family culture around health and decisions about accessing external health care. This may have provided a template for learning about what it means to be ill and when it is acceptable to be unwell or have time off from responsibilities. Such learning can have a bearing upon future health behaviours of the A/N individual.

PREVIOUSLY LEARNT ATTITUDES AFFECT YOUR HEALTH NOW

Health behaviours are what each of us do regarding health-related issues. They can include taking a break, using medication (over-the-counter or prescribed), doing exercises shown by a physiotherapist, going for X-rays or having surgery. Additionally, the messages around health that people identify as being appropriate and or correct can impact directly upon decisions and behaviours related to one's health. It is therefore important for each of us to take some time to reflect upon the messages we have picked up over time and that may now guide our health-related behaviour.

The fact you are reading this book indicates you have at least some degree of identification with the A/N personality-style. As such, you may have picked up some attitudes and expectations around health over the years and these could possibly be guiding some of your behaviours and self-care approaches. If you can start to account for the potential impact of these early messages, there may be opportunities to better influence your health when necessary. However, it is also important to understand that such benefits are not just physical; they can have positive spin-offs for psychological welfare and general quality of life as well. It may also have future financial benefit for you as you start to consider the benefits of 'preventive maintenance' for your body. Staving off a heart attack or reducing blood pressure surely has considerable benefits for the future of both you and your family. It may also mean that you can continue working rather than having to prematurely retire or leave your job due to health issues. If you would like to make positive changes and challenge unhelpful health behaviours and attitudes, you may benefit from understanding the schemas and beliefs that promote certain ways of viewing and responding to your own health. By gaining an understanding of how these attitudes have impacted your way of caring for yourself, you will be better placed to understand when these are coming into play and therefore be able to choose options rather than automatically following a well-practised approach.

If you consider what you have read so far in this book, you may start to see that attitudes about what is 'correct' and 'expected' for health can have an impact on physical and psychological welfare. Some of the key schemas within the A/N individual can be concerned with getting on with things, potentially not letting pain or illness affect responsibilities, and the primacy of your work. These are powerful scripts to operate by. The primacy of your work can mean that one's own needs are relegated to the background. For the business executive there may be demands within the work day, an important contract that needs finetuning or ensuring that employee needs are met, and these may well take precedence over personal health status.

Obviously a wide range of factors can and do influence health status. Part of this is our genetic make-up that we were given right from the start. Although there is not much we can do about our genetic inheritance, there may be options for us to better manage how we respond to what our genes might throw at us. If we can see that the health-related behaviours we undertake are modifiable, we may have an opportunity to reduce the impact of health problems or gain better outcomes from treatment. The important aspect for each of us is to realize that the decisions we take at any stage of the health cycle will be affected by the way each of us makes sense of and relates to what it means to be an A/N person. If you strongly relate to the A/N style of interacting with the world, you will be more likely to overlook minor ailments and less likely to find time to consult a doctor. The former may be due to the nuisance value of addressing non-urgent issues while the latter may be difficult due to competing demands such as work pressures and timing of appointments.

The degree that one 'lives' the A/N life may map indirectly onto healthcare use and the value placed on caring for oneself. If you are busy with work, family or sport (and their associated demanding schedules) there may be little room to engage in the aforementioned 'preventive maintenance'. Once the A/N person is caught up in their world, the expectations and beliefs of the associated culture may override the needs of the physical self. Indeed, there may be a very low level of tolerance for taking days off due to illness when there are plans to implement and tasks to complete. Once these external aspects are mapped onto the internalized expectations and beliefs, the stage is set for a long-term process of potentially riding through minor ailments, putting off consultations and clinical tests as well as not having time to comply with treatment regimes. Such beliefs are often magnified by the ethos and expectations of the environment you operate in. If this is in a competitive workplace (think promotions, bonuses and achieving partnerships), there may be a significant amount of modelling around health behaviours. As one ascends the professional ladder, it will be noticed if time is taken off due to illness. If deadlines need to be extended, there may be personal, work-related or even financial repercussions.

In some ways, the A/N person may be a victim of their own process as far as awareness of health status goes. By not attending the doctor very often, the assumption is that all is well and the person is healthy. This can be a self-sustaining issue that has implications when s/he does finally attend a health clinic. The individual may overlook other physical challenges that are not (yet) too problematic, as they wish to get the current issue addressed and return to what they are doing as quickly as possible. This is consistent with the A/N personality-style, which tends to favour the 'here and now' over the future and is more oriented to the goal rather than the process. So you may find yourself attending the doctor, describing an issue and then seeking the quickest intervention, such as oral medication, to address the problem rather than listening to or complying with changes to diet, exercise or general health-management advice. From the other side of the desk, the clinician may be at risk of operating on a form of shorthand due to your history of attendance and possible minimization of symptoms. This can set up a 'false positive' paradigm where both patient and clinician see the encounter within the context of a healthy person. One of the dangers of this is that consultations tend to be shorter, fewer questions are asked and fewer preventive options provided. This is not necessarily because the doctor is uncaring or not doing their job. Rather, it can be a consequence of the history around attendance, the minimization of problems and symptoms (by the A/N patient) and the limited time available in consultations. For both parties, the assumption of wellness can mean certain courses of action are favoured over others.

CASE STUDY

Benjamin is a busy professional who made one of his few visits to the doctor after having trouble breathing when training for a half-marathon. He gave a cursory account of the difficulties within the specific confines of the running environment and shared with the doctor his self-diagnosis of 'exercise-induced asthma'. Benjamin then proceeded to explain to the doctor that his preferred approach would be to get an inhaler to deal with the symptoms when training. As someone who didn't like attending healthcare professionals and begrudgingly admitted to viewing health problems as a personal failure, Benjamin wanted to get the problem sorted and return to his running.

The doctor offered the opinion that the symptoms were 'not too convincing of asthma', yet he acquiesced and provided the sought-after inhaler. This seems to have been a situation where one party was bringing certain A/N expectations and pressures to the consultation and this, when combined with the general presumption of good health (as crudely measured by attendance rates at the doctor) resulted in a treatment approach not necessarily favoured by the doctor. In due course, Benjamin was back at the doctor with worsening symptoms that resulted in a referral to a cardiologist, with subsequent stenting being carried out!

Minimizing problems

Of course, it is a tall ask of the medical fraternity to identify a patient as operating within an A/N manner. More so to expect them to immediately realize that the way such a patient has learnt to go about things will probably affect their descriptions of symptoms and timing of presentation. Therefore, it is important that you, the A/N person, develop an understanding of factors relevant to how you view health and how you behave in response to your changing health status.

I don't think it would be fair or appropriate to say that the A/N individual does not care about their health. Similarly, it is probably not the case that, deep down, you are convinced that you are bullet-proof and super-human in terms of health. It is more likely that a range of A/N-type schemas are operating that make it less likely that you will go to the doctor. These include the earlier mentioned aspects, but it is helpful to note that these may also be layered onto internal factors such as a tendency towards minimization, a degree of denial and not wishing to be seen as 'not in control'.

The tendency to minimize problems is an interesting trait and one that can map easily onto the A/N personality-style. It can perhaps be best seen as a coping strategy (albeit not always a helpful one) which is designed to underline a sense of being in control. If health issues are downplayed, this can be a way of ensuring that one does not overreact or — worse still — be *seen* to be overreacting to physical problems. Thus, cardiac symptoms might be explained away as representing asthma or indigestion problems. This reduces the psychological conflict around the person needing to be available for work but perhaps also wondering about consulting a doctor.

However, in the medium to long term, this minimization is not useful or helpful. The real-life outcome can be that you encounter internal barriers to seeking timely and effective help. This can have consequences for yourself, your family, your workplace and the medical personnel who try to treat the problem when you do eventually attend for assistance. Invariably, the condition will have worsened or advanced, which can have implications for cost, time off work and prognosis. So minimization may well end up a rather costly strategy! If we stay with the case study involving cardiac symptoms, the implications for the status of the arteries and the potential for experiencing a heart attack may be significant — not taking your symptoms seriously can have direct effects on future wellbeing and employment. I therefore encourage anyone with the A/N traits described here to ask themselves: 'Why do I not go to the doctor?', 'Am I prioritizing work over my health?', 'What is behind my tendency to minimize my symptoms?' It is perhaps time to look in the mirror and ask yourself honestly about what might be getting in the way of caring for yourself. It is possible that the reasons are rooted within the A/N approach to life.

. . . .

As you can see, an A/N personality-style potentially impacts health status. This is not to say that this is a defining characteristic of the A/N person. Rather, it is yet another component of life that is affected by this far-reaching personality-style. It is probably true that some aspects of the A/N personality-style are more relevant than others. Further, it would also be true that some people who identify with the A/N approach to life do prioritize their health status and care. This can be because good health is seen as vital to achieving the goal/s they are most focused upon, for example in the case of marathon runners. So it may be more about understanding when some aspects of the A/N personality-style are coming into play and also seeing how and when these affect decision making. How the A/N person makes sense of their internal demands, and how they see the expectations of those around them (the boss and other hard-working people) regarding health issues, will have an effect upon the health-related behaviours they choose.

A final issue of physical relevance for the A/N individual is the tendency to believe their body will inform them when they have reached their tolerance level. Unfortunately, such people can become so focused on the goal that they ignore, override, misinterpret or generally discount changes to the way they are feeling. This can see them pushing on despite the fact the body is providing feedback that things are under stress or being affected. In its simplest form, this might be the development of a cold or feeling fatigued. However, at the other end of the spectrum this can be a significant illness or disease process. Unfortunately, many A/N people only notice the feedback from their body — and take it as a message that something is wrong — when they struggle to carry on. Only then do they seem to consider that something might be affecting them or is out of balance. However, most probably there has been a feedback loop operating from the body for quite some time. It just hasn't been attended to . . . time to change this, perhaps?

PSYCHOLOGICAL HEALTH

There are a number of aspects related to psychological health. In terms of the A/N personality-style we will explore depression and anxiety.

Depression

It is not unusual for people who push themselves to experience alterations to their mood. As the demands of work or general life build up, there can be implications for how people feel about themselves and a particular situation. Within the general population, depression is a relatively common disorder. It is, however, a truth that depression is not always recognized by many of the people involved, including the individuals themselves, the doctor who may be consulted and family members and friends. This can particularly occur with those who might be termed 'high functioning' depressed people — a group that could well include more than its fair share of A/N individuals.

Every human experiences a range of emotions and this includes low mood due to frustrations, losses and upsetting events. Some of these lowered moods may be characterized more appropriately as sadness and grief, while others might be more of a reactive lowering in response to events. On top of this, though, there can be what is termed a major depressive episode. This is a clinical condition involving a lowered mood that is present nearly every day and can be accompanied by a reduced interest in usually enjoyable activities and a drop in motivation.

Alongside this, there can be a range of physical effects that are associated with the condition. In more pronounced cases, this may also result in thoughts about death and self-harm. This is by no means a full and complete checklist for major depression but it gives an idea of some of the changes that come about when a person's mood lowers consistently.

There is no single reason or event that results in or causes depression in everyone that experiences it. Indeed, there can be a range of events and situations that contribute components to the significant change in mood for an individual. These may be a genetic vulnerability (a family history traced through a number of sufferers) and/or the presence of stressful events such as work, relationship and financial issues. Such issues can be compounded by a change in thinking style that accompanies lowered mood and results in the person adopting a more negative view of life and events.

Depression is not a 'one size fits all' problem. So if this condition is relevant, you might need some help to make sense of what is happening for you and some advice on the options available. One of the most important messages for anyone who has an A/N personality-style is that depression is not a failing, nor is it indicative of weakness. I point this out as most A/N individuals have issues around control and a fear of failure. Associated with this is a mistaken view within general society that only 'weak' people become depressed. As a practising clinical psychologist, I can assure you that people from all walks of life and socio-economic backgrounds present with mood-related challenges.

There is no singly identifiable person who presents with this condition, and it is neither fair nor accurate to describe depressed people as being weak-willed or having a compromised character. People with very responsible positions in large organizations have struggled with their mood. It is also important for you to know that most people recover sufficiently from a depressive episode to return to their general lives.

An appropriate first port of call would be to talk with your family doctor. Remember, that there is no need to feel shame at becoming depressed. As we have seen, there are a range of reasons why this can develop. For the A/N person, these may include the continuous pressures and stressors of performing at high levels in their chosen field. Alongside this may have been the constant presence of that unhelpful passenger or critic that has freely imparted negative messages about performance and ability in general. It is a truth that even healthy, fit and dedicated people can wear themselves out, both physically and psychologically.

If your partner or doctor has identified changes to your mood, it may be time to pause and listen. As noted, the first step is to see a professional who can help with the diagnosis and provide either direct assistance or a referral to another professional with appropriate specialist training. There are also any number of self-help books available from bookshops as well as websites (and material available from these). A complete discussion around the role of anti-depressants is beyond the scope of this book. However, I would like you to be open to talking through all options with your medical or mental health professional if the need arises. By fully informing yourself about all options, you will hopefully be better placed to make the decisions about your health and welfare that you need to make.

There is a significant body of research-based evidence around the benefits of the talking-based therapies for mood problems. One of the best known approaches within this is Cognitive Behavioural Therapy (CBT), which helps you understand the factors that have contributed to the current depressive episode while providing a range of strategies to manage your symptoms. For our purposes, it is important to understand that pushing yourself (both physically and mentally) while being hard on yourself and dismissive of achievements can have a detrimental effect upon your mood. This, in turn, can undermine your confidence and impact your performance in the role you value so highly. Hopefully, by understanding the key issues within this chapter and developing an awareness of signs and symptoms that indicate your mood is lowering, you may be able to respond positively and in a timely manner to prevent the problems compounding and making things increasingly difficult for you.

Anxiety

The other issue of potential relevance to A/N people is the presence of anxiety. This can lurk around in the shadows of depression and quietly sneak up, or be a challenge within its own right. This condition is about being 'not sure' and includes quite a few questions of the 'What if…?' type. This is important for the A/N individual as anxiety can result in the person second-guessing themself and living in a heightened state of arousal, where the worst-case scenario seems the most obvious outcome. It tends to undermine an individual's sense of control and may reinforce the nagging doubts that maybe, just maybe 'I am a fraud after all'.

Anxiety is a busy condition indeed. It has several components that can have a specific or cumulative effect on the individual. These are: an emotional response; a physical response; unhelpful and worrying thoughts; and also changes to how we behave (i.e. we tend to avoid the things we are anxious about). Anxiety is a basic defence mechanism that developed in humans a long time ago, when we were living in caves and eating woolly mammoth steaks for dinner. It is essentially about keeping ourselves safe by quickly getting ready for threats within our world. The aim of it is to rev up the system to respond to a potential threat. It does this by getting the body ready to either do battle with the threat or hot-foot it away from the scene of the threat. This is known as the fight or flight response, which produces useful physical changes that assist us to deal with the threat. Most noticeably, the fight or flight response involves pumping blood to the major muscle groups to give them oxygen in readiness for action. As part of this, our breathing becomes faster (and shallower) and our heart rate increases alongside a tensing of certain muscle groups. By doing this, and by releasing adrenaline, the person has a better chance of responding to a threat and hopefully looking after themselves. These responses are common throughout the animal kingdom and, let's face it, we humans are also animals when all is said and done.

This defence mechanism was designed for a simpler, more physical age but we still carry it with us in the 21st century. It is still necessary and not something you can completely rid yourself of — so don't waste your time and energy trying. But while eliminating anxiety is a bridge too far, managing it is definitely possible.

Have you noticed how our world has become more complex, socialized and technologically driven? This means that with the busy brains we have developed, we can now get anxious about things that are not physical threats; in fact, the 'threat' does not even have to be associated with immediate events. Our specialized brains have enabled us to imagine and project ahead, or back, in time. This means that we can become anxious about social interactions and potential difficulties and threats. The relevance of this to the A/N group is that humans can become anxious about potential failure and the potential responses of others to our (perceived) failings and poor performances. Anxiety becomes more of a problem when we anticipate future events or problems and when such concerns become consistent or second nature. This results in an ongoing state of heightened emotional, physical and cognitive arousal, which is not helpful or efficient.

As noted, our systems respond in this manner whether the danger is real or perceived. The individual becomes increasingly alert and starts to scan the environment (physical or social) for variations of the threat, and for any new ones. Because our system is then primed for action, it doesn't take much to trigger a response of fleeing or responding in an attacking manner. Within a social setting, this can see an anxious person leave the environment or say something they may later regret. Due to the fact the alarm system is ringing loud and clear, the focus is on dealing with the perceived threat and not much thought goes into the consequences of our actions. This can be costly in an employment situation where one may verbally attack another due to the perceived threat — not good if the recipient is your boss!

When anxious, our thinking becomes less sophisticated with a much narrower focus (i.e. dealing with the threatening situation that is here and now). The thoughts are around being in some kind of 'danger' and we tend to consider the worst-case scenario regarding the outcome. This is important for the A/N individual as you can 'learn' that unfamiliar situations, such as not meeting a goal or deadline, are threatening. This can result in an increase in effort and energy expenditure beyond the already high levels, in order to stave off potential failure. Alternatively, it might result in further procrastination or avoidance.

Living in a state of uncertainty and wondering if or when things will go wrong will quietly but surely wind up the nervous system, undermine confidence and potentially heighten the fear of failure that may be lurking beneath the surface.

BURN-OUT: THE A/N PERSON'S NEMESIS

The concept and indeed identification of burn-out is nothing new. Companies have been aware of this for decades and the industrial and organizational arms of psychology have studied and written much about this. Burn-out is often seen as an ailment of the corporate world in the 20th century and beyond. In essence, it is a personal response to regularly engaging in high-demand situations over extended periods. It is yet another multidimensional concept but one that tends to have some key components to it. It is important to realise that burn-out is no respecter of age, gender or salary bracket. It is also not restricted to the employment situation and can, for example, be seen in the performing arts as well as sporting arenas. Thus, individuals from across the spectrum can be vulnerable to this.

People suffering from burn-out tend to evaluate their performance more negatively and have also been noted to exhibit higher levels of perfectionism. Such individuals (prior to or early on in their decline) tend to work harder and harder to obtain the approval of others and avoid additional negative impacts on how they view themselves and their performance. This is, unfortunately, a bit like wildly thrashing about in deep mud — it gives the impression that one is doing something to solve the dilemma but, in fact, only makes the problem worse (and messier). Part of the problem can be a fear within the individual that they will be perceived as weak if they acknowledge feeling stressed or that they will be seen as unable to cope. As time passes, the person may actually take on more tasks in order to prove there is no problem, which invariably compounds the difficulties. Within the world of athletics, this can see the person training for longer hours or aiming for better times — despite the fact they are feeling overwhelmed.

Signs of change towards the unhelpful might have been present for some time but no one has been willing to openly identify it, be it an employer, a colleague, a partner or the person themselves. People on the road to burn-out are progressively lacking in energy and become increasingly dissatisfied with their work life. As a result of the demands on them, and an ever-increasing sense of tiredness, the person tends to rely on less effective coping strategies, which means they can become less effective at problem solving, saying no to people and balancing the demands of work. There is also increasing evidence that living under stress can impair the performance of the prefrontal cortex, which is that part of the brain involved with strategizing and grasping the overall scene as opposed to the issue right in front of you. Without this higher-order thinking happening, one is at risk of 'dumbing down' responses and making less smart decisions. Over time, the unfinished work tasks tend to pile up and the individual feels like s/he will never get to the end, which can have a significant effect on both the sense of self and mood levels. Similarly, for a concert violinist, this may involve being less enthusiastic about rehearsals or completing the required practice at home before the performance.

At the core of burn-out is a sense of emotional tiring or exhaustion. This comes about due to the ongoing nature of job demands and pressures, where the individual is consistently operating at a level that requires more from them emotionally than is being replenished. Alongside this is a type of intellectual or cognitive tiredness that presents itself as a loss of sharpness and reduced ability to do the previously normal cognitive tasks required of the person in a given position. There is a lessening of physical and personal energy available to the role in contrast to what the person previously brought to (and demonstrated within) their job, sporting event or artistic endeavour.

Perhaps one of the most problematic aspects of this condition is the creeping sense of dissatisfaction that can ultimately lead to cynicism. Such cynicism can be about the role itself, the company worked for, the sporting competitions aimed for, or even about the individual themselves — who they are, what they have achieved and where they are heading. It's a bit like an existential train wreck, something that calls into question the very foundation of the person and how they have been operating. It is important to see that burn-out is not an adjustment of previously held beliefs and attitudes. It tends to be more than this and one can see a pendulum-like effect where the person goes from being very engaged and energized through to pulling back, not sharing the values of the organization and distancing themselves from colleagues. Remember, though, that this is not just about business executives. The challenges and negative outcomes can present themselves to people who are focused on achieving at a (consistently) high level in demanding roles that are important to them. Similar patterns of responding can be seen in academic researchers who have been pursuing an academic goal for years, and a runner who has to repetitively do high mileage on a regular basis to stand a chance of moving up through the rankings.

Clearly, burn-out is problematic and challenging. It is also a condition that causes many problems and can cost those involved lots of money due to decreased performance, poor focus and reduced engagement in the collective goals of the group or organization one is involved in, which ultimately results in declining outcomes. The lack of performance comes about due to the person becoming overwhelmed and disengaged; they tend to find it hard to see the point of making an effort and striving for goals. This, of course, leads to reduced accomplishment that can flow on to a sense of personal incompetence and reduced sense of self-efficacy. Alongside this is a reduction in commitment to projects and goals, plus an ever increasing sense of dissatisfaction with the role. This often results in a desire to leave; however, this can be a less-than-focused process. Often, it is an undifferentiated (and drawn out) experience of changeable moods and disillusionment, whereby the person feels lousy but can't always figure out why. As a result, plans to address the problem are often not very clear and this can lead to a period of cognitive wandering and imagining of options for a better life; but problem-solving action does not necessarily follow. Just how does one leave a symphony orchestra after many years of striving to be chosen for such a competitive position? Thus, the period of poor performance is stretched out and the costs maximized. This is problematic as the person may then start to pull back and perform poorly in other spheres of their life. Their energy, both physical and cognitive, is depleted and they begin to experience changed patterns and quality of sleep, have poorer self-rated health status and may develop higher levels of cardiovascular disease. Another serious complaint they may experience is that of lowered mood and depression.

Who's at risk?

It is important to understand that burn-out is not inevitable. Nor is it guaranteed to affect all people who have busy jobs or are engaged in a demanding, high-level pursuit. There are some differences that make certain individuals more vulnerable to develop and then remain susceptible to burn-out. Thus, having a strong work ethic may not, in itself, be the key determinant of developing such problems. The work of van Beek and colleagues (2012) may be relevant in this respect and also help us identify why the A/N individual can be vulnerable to experiencing burn-out. The authors distinguish between two types of working hard. They identify positive attributes associated with 'work engagement' and the more negative attributes of the 'workaholic'. One of the key differences between these two types of people concerns motivation and self-regulation. The workaholic is more strongly influenced by external forces, while work engagement relates to intrinsic motivation. The workaholic is that person who never seems to go home, and can (and will) do everything in the office. People tend to describe workaholics as unusually dedicated and machine-like. This is not so much for their robotic demeanour but, rather, their readiness to do more and to keep going. The question for our purposes is whether the A/N personality-style fits neatly into one of these categories (engaged worker or workaholic), is an amalgam of the two or perhaps even begins within one arena and shifts over time to the other.

According to van Beek, workaholics tend to be obsessed with work and push themselves continuously. A point to note is that such individuals usually work harder than is needed in terms of the expectations on them. Outside of the workplace, performance arena or sports stadium they remain focused on the role and experience an inner drive to work hard that they perhaps do not fully understand or have control over. Alongside this approach is a range of less-than-positive outcomes for the individual relating to enjoyment of life and relationships, and a poor balance between work and home. Where the workaholic tends not to derive great satisfaction from their role, the engaged individual seems to run on keenness, enthusiasm and pride in their role. Underlying this is a real sense of investment in the work role and van Beek talks about this engaged group being 'pulled to work'. When looked at closely, they may actually be more efficient and productive than their workaholic counterparts, so long hours by themselves do not equate with efficient outcomes and high production.

As noted above, an engaged worker has an intrinsic motivation, which in essence means they find the role interesting and enjoyable and therefore engage in it for its own sake. In contrast, says van Beek, the extrinsically motivated person undertakes the role and maintains it due to the potential outcome of the task rather than the task itself. The authors further note that extrinsically motivated people are responsive to external costs and outcomes — that is, they work hard to avoid criticism. Such people also seem to obtain and maintain feelings of self-worth by meeting the standards they feel other, significant people expect. If they do not meet these standards, they reportedly experience self-criticism and develop a sense of not being up to the task. It is interesting to note that workaholics experience negative feelings such as anxiety, shame and guilt if they do not work hard. Also, it seems that such workers believe that others hold high standards for them and that they will only be accepted if they meet these standards, even if they are not clearly defined or articulated. So there are some notable similarities between this description and how A/N people tend to operate. It is this internal pressure to work that van Beek suggests is associated with workaholism and, subsequently, burn-out. Such factors and ways of behaving are clearly seen within the A/N population and these people tend to operate in the same manner as the workaholic. We therefore have some strong indicators that the A/N individual is at heightened risk of burn-out and the associated emotional and physical costs.

The job made me do it

Although there are many professions in which A/N people work, there are some that likely attract a higher proportion of such people. One group is the legal profession, where tradition, doing things correctly and working very hard is valued. It would seem that to rise through the ranks, one must demonstrate dedication to the cause and a willingness to work long hours, often beyond those one is actually employed for. I recall speaking with a friend when he was practising law in the United States. He would describe that he had finally finished his work around 2 a.m. and there was little point in heading home as, following his commute, he would no sooner be settled into sleep than he'd need to get up again to travel back to start his next day. He also described the expectations for new employees: that they would commit themselves to the firm and its aims. Interestingly, this was not necessarily articulated but it soon became apparent to new employees by watching the behaviours of the partners and other senior lawyers. When I asked what would happen to a new person who did not demonstrate their abilities by undertaking long hours, I was told that nothing would actively happen to them but they would probably not advance within the firm. Now, what are the chances that this unarticulated, informal message would go unnoticed?

Hopkins and Gardner (2012) provide some insights to the legal profession. They identify that, as a group, lawyers are impacted by psychological distress to a greater level than both the general population and other occupational groups. The authors wonder whether personality traits prevalent among lawyers may make them more vulnerable to such issues as depression and anxiety. The personality traits they identify include perfectionism and a need for achievement, which, as we have seen, form part of the A/N personality-style. The imbalance between work and personal life discussed earlier is also noted by Hopkins and Gardner as being common in the legal profession, and is also regularly identified as one of the predictors of burn-out, as is the presence of psychological distress.

Certain personality types are perhaps pulled towards jobs that are demanding and require a dedication to the cause. Hopkins and Gardner note that the individuals *less* likely to experience burn-out are those who identify positively with their role. This is consistent with the findings of van Beek and colleagues, who describe the 'engaged worker' as being at less risk of burn-out. As discussed earlier, the A/N personality-style is more akin to the workaholic than the engaged worker. However, if such people can begin to shift the emphasis within their lives from achieving for achievement's sake and replace this with a desire to do a good job in a satisfying and *sustainable* manner, this can reduce the risk of burn-out for the A/N person.

One of the messages from this chapter for the A/N reader may therefore be that there are risks to focusing on the outcomes alone, particularly in the long term Hopefully, you are starting to see that how you operate can have an effect on your health — both physical and psychological — and that it may be time to make some changes so that you can save yourself from yourself.

IN SUMMARY

The A/N approach to life is somewhat of a double-edged sword. It clearly brings about achievements and positive outcomes but can also have costs. As some of these are delayed, you might not notice they are building up. As the A/N person tends to focus on the project or task at hand, s/he tends not to look ahead and this can limit the ability to care for oneself. There can also be competing demands from prioritized tasks such as work, which can delay individuals seeking help with health problems. Attitudes to caring for yourself may have been developed over time, such as within the family, and these early messages can impact decisions taken later in life.

Part of being an A/N individual is having a low tolerance to things that don't work out. If you see health problems as a failing, or that addressing these is an acknowledgement of being weak, then your chances of actively addressing health problems is lessened. Minimizing your symptoms and problems will not make them go away; in fact, it may well make things harder in the longer term. If you relate to this pattern, now is the time to start rebalancing things in your life. After all, you can't excel in your chosen field if the body is not able to perform as well as it can. It may therefore be helpful to pause and reflect upon what is behind the health choices you have been making.

Health issues, illness, depression and anxiety are *not* failures. You are human, despite your strengths and achievements. Ask yourself: what other machine have you run (often at peak performance) every day for 30, 40, 50 or more years? Do you expect all the machinery and devices you have purchased to last for this length of time without demonstrating some problems or needing some servicing?

Burn-out is a state of not having the energy or enthusiasm to do what you previously loved being involved with. You may notice it as a distancing (psychologically and physically) from your role. It doesn't just happen to one 'type' of person. Rather, there may well be some similarities within the people that experience burn-out, not the least of which are pushing yourself to attain goals while being concerned about judgments from others and only feeling good when you meet that target you set. If you are struggling in your chosen role and find that your sense of self is precariously balanced or dependant on feedback from others, you may well be at risk of experiencing burn-out. Maybe it is time to do some things for their own sake, not because they fit in with some greater goal.

ASPECTS FOR REFLECTION, OPTIONS FOR CHANGE

Being yourself — rather than who you think you should be or feel you are expected to be — is an important step in managing your health. If you act in ways that feel real and genuine for you, it is more likely you will be accounting for important aspects of your wellbeing. There is a strong relationship between happiness, feeling less stressed, doing well at work and living in a style that is consistent with your personal values rather than one which simply fits with your goals.

In terms of your overall self, take some time to consider how you relate to your physical wellbeing and health. Ask yourself what's behind the decisions you take and have taken about your health. Why are you putting off going to the doctor for a check-up? What might be the long-term outcome of such behaviours, for you, your career, your partner or your children?

What if you started to work with your body and its needs, rather than fighting it or just pushing it?

What if you started to view your doctor in a similar vein as your business mentor or sporting coach, as someone who can provide advice or help you address problems that may be undermining your progress, rather than someone you only go to once your body has 'failed' or broken down.

What if you took a risk with your usual health behaviours and booked an appointment to find out just what that nagging cough is about or why the spot on your shoulder has turned black?

In terms of your psychological health, be assured that it is possible to expand your repertoire of management strategies. However, the first step is to realize you may be facing a challenge. If you can relate to the symptoms of anxiety or depression listed earlier in the chapter, *now* is the time to do something about them. If you are not sure, show this chapter to your partner, best friend or a family member and ask them if they think the symptoms are relevant to you. Below are some specific things you can do right now.

- Talk with someone in the first instance, such as a family member or friend.
- Consult your family doctor.
- Be open to the option of medications (e.g. antidepressants) if advised.

- Consider participating in some talking therapy (e.g. CBT) with a psychologist.
- Learn more about stress management and how to enhance any strategies you currently have in place. There are many good self-help books available, or you could talk with an accredited counsellor or psychologist. Skills they can help you with include: problem-solving approaches, options for dealing with unhelpful cognitions (worry), diaphragmatic breathing, relaxation techniques, meditation, mindfulness skills, Tai Chi (it's okay, men, the moves were originally martial arts techniques!).
- Check out relevant professional websites about depression and anxiety.

Burn-out is not inevitable. Part of the secret to keeping it at bay relates to your motivation for the task and where it comes from. There are protective aspects to being motivated by your own reasons and values rather than by external factors or payoffs. If you are working towards goals and outcomes that are relevant and consistent with your values (more about values later), there is less chance that you will become overwhelmed and then burn out. This intrinsic drive and reasoning will help you sustain effort when things get tough, as the goals are consistent with who you are and what is important to you — that is, they are not simply related to reinforcers such as increased money or respect from others. There is also an association between intrinsically identified goals and enhanced feelings of personal wellbeing, sense of self and confidence for doing things.

So what is it that drives you in your current role: to do the best job you can, or to be famous? And where does the reinforcement come from: within you, or from other people or things outside of you?

Try this

Grab a pen and paper. Make a list of as many things as you can that motivate you or act as payoffs/reinforcers in the key domain you are exploring (e.g. employment/career, family, sport). Now go down this list and write beside each item either an 'I' for an internal motivator or reinforcer and an 'E' for an external one. Count them up and see which predominates. What does this show you, and what might it suggest about your approach to this particular activity?

. . . .

Following on from the above reflection exercise, it may be interesting to consider how this behaviour sits with who you are and what is important to you. Is there a close fit between the way you have been behaving in this key domain and what is truly important to you? Or have things become unbalanced? If the exercise suggests you are motivated by external factors and payoffs, could this be driving you in a direction or to an extent that is starting to clash with what is meaningful to you? Maybe, over time, you have lost the sense of what is central to and fulfilling for you as an individual. Remember, burn-out is more likely if you are driving yourself for external reasons and to attain outcomes that are not necessarily central to the real you.

Ask yourself: what is needed to help you *engage* with your work role rather than be enslaved by it? It might be time to check in with your attitude and understanding around your role and efforts regarding your chosen pursuit. Is there a gap, or perhaps even a chasm, between how you initially envisioned yourself behaving and what you are actually doing at this point?

If you are approaching and then engaging with your role in a way that fits closely with your true interests and desires, there is a greater likelihood that you will have a fulfilling relationship with the role. As a result, it may also be more enjoyable and sustainable for you. However, if your role has been dominating your life to the point where other previously enjoyed activities have disappeared, something is not gelling.

Try this

In order to make some change to this sphere of your life, consider just what was the original motivation for you in relation to your current role and your performance in it. Write down the answers to the following questions.

- What drew you towards this role or activity in the first place?
- Why and how closely did this initially fit with your personal desires and values?
- Is there anything about the way you currently approach your role or activity that could be changed so that it might fit more closely with your personal desires and values?

Helpful hint: If you are an employer or supervisor, be aware that role and workload can be perceived either as a taxing demand or a positive challenge by your employees and colleagues. As you can see from this chapter, what an individual brings to the workplace or team environment can have a significant bearing on their ability to cope with the tasks set for them. It may be advantageous to consider this when selecting individuals for roles in your organization. If you select people whose values, aptitudes and skills (not just conscientious behaviour) are congruent with the role in question, this should help them positively identify with the role. Therefore, they may be more likely to engage with the role rather than feel dominated or stressed by it. As a result, they may find that they enjoy their role more, and this can often translate to better performance (plus reduce the chance of burn-out) — surely a win–win situation.

· · · · · · · · · · · · · · · · · · · ·

As you understand more about the A/N approach to life and consider making some positive changes, think about this: what if you tried to shape your career-related behaviours around a refreshed, more meaningful approach to life . . . as opposed to shaping your life around your career?

8 New perspectives, achievement and the 'me'

Change is central to adaptation and the successful mastery of a situation or environment. As Darwin pointed out many years ago, it is the species that adapts to the demands of the environment that stands the best chance of carrying on. In order to make the most of one's opportunities, the individual needs to adapt to changes or new expectations in the environment, whether this be the workplace, your wider career or relationships.

However, to see (and therefore benefit from) alternatives, we must be able to shift perspective when needed. Perhaps even more useful is the ability to weigh up options and then implement the most advantageous response. The opposite approach revolves around perseveration of ideas and behaviours, which can lead to a sense of 'stuckness' and, in the extreme, learned helplessness, when you have the sense that there is no point trying any more because nothing seems to work.

In essence, adaptability is about choosing the most useful response at a given time, one that maximizes your chances of coping with the situational demands with minimal drain on your resources. Thus, you can adapt and adjust as needed without just relying on a 'full on' or 'full off' response set.

As we have seen already, the default option of the A/N person to challenging situations is to respond with a set of behaviours that revolve around putting in more hours and demanding more of themselves. If this sounds like you, it is possible you are identifying a bit too much with your tried and true methods, which can lead to an overdeveloped belief in their usefulness. In such situations, you may find yourself acting on autopilot. This can result in you no longer actively considering how things are shaping up or changing; you experience a narrowing of focus. This may then impact your ability to monitor and regulate the extent of your dedication to the task.

If such an approach is relentlessly followed but results do not eventuate, it can have negative implications for the sense of self. So, for the A/N person, a 'management' option often used is to move away from the task or issue that is threatening to the individual's sense of accomplishment. It seems safer to no longer engage in an activity than be confronted with a deteriorating sense of self. This narrowing of repertoire and responses can be further accentuated when the A/N person encounters potential criticism. The internal critic (with his/her harsh language) can start to dominate attention and also the person's emotional space. With increased processing of emotional responding, there is less energy for more useful and adaptive responses to the actual problem at hand. As we become wrapped up in negative thoughts and feelings, we will start to struggle with the extent of these feelings. We may also find it hard to shift focus to what is needed (here and now) in order to bring about a positive resolution. In these situations, it seems that the focus is more upon the outcome than considering how to modify or adjust the process used.

HOW DO I START TO CHANGE?

'I know that I need to change, but I don't have time to.'
Emily, 38, business owner

One of the ways for the A/N person to shift from this well-rehearsed approach is to learn to tolerate feelings and thoughts that either drive them beyond their tolerance levels or promote a sense that they need to give up on a task. The internal critic might actually work to your advantage if you can tolerate the thoughts and channel the emotions from this internal feedback into a more useful approach. Within this, if you can learn to tone down the criticism and reframe the messages as a more motivational, supportively challenging voice, you could potentially engage in more effective problem solving.

By learning to better tolerate the strong emotions that arise when confronted by a lack of progress or outcome, you can become more flexible with your approaches and also be able to adapt more readily. It may be beneficial for you to consider things from differing angles, such that you can attain a new perspective on the event that confronts you. If you can become aware of a task's current demands and how they might be different to previous activities, you may be able to tap into higher-order processing related to available options, rather than recycling behaviours that can limit available choices.

One branch of the psychological therapies that promotes this flexibility as being central to a healthy existence is Acceptance and Commitment Therapy, or ACT. This very practical and useful approach endeavours to take account of the context for an individual and their behaviours. An introduction to this approach is contained in a 2006 paper by Hayes and his colleagues. One of their aims is to help the person build a wider repertoire of coping options, with an emphasis on flexibility. This school of thought emphasizes that when we get too involved with and wrapped up in our thoughts, we risk controlling our behaviour through pre-existing rules and the thoughts themselves. By behaving like this, A/N people may end up acting (automatically) in a way that is consistent with a strong focus on achievement at all cost, and miss out on the bigger picture that offers some balance and flexibility. This is certainly representative of the A/N individual in that s/he may live an increasingly narrow life that, over time, unwittingly distances them from the things they previously held to be important. The goals, tasks and requirements of their professional role and associated projects take precedence. As a result, the person tends to rely increasingly on a restricted number of approaches to life and its problems (e.g. you push yourself harder as that is what is 'expected'). One of the things I consider useful about the ACT approach is that it tries to reconnect people with the things that are truly important to them. Within this, the approach tries to help the person align their behaviour so it is consistent with and guided by their values, so that the person moves toward wider ranging, more positive benefits from their actions.

There may well be room for you, as an A/N person, to reconnect with personal values so that you can push back the limits of the overly focused approach to life and career. Similarly, by disengaging from the intensity and direction of the thoughts, you may find the messages from the unhelpful inner critic to be less believable and therefore exert less control over your decisions and actions. It may also have benefits for the sense of personal embarrassment sometimes experienced and the negative (self-generated) put-downs that A/N people tend to endure.

GOALS DRIVE YOU BUT VALUES CAN GUIDE YOU

Values are those aspects an individual feels are important in terms of direction in life, and perhaps what they wish their life to be about or would like it to reflect. If these can be clarified for the

A/N person, then the values might operate as signposts for life, particularly during times when the journey becomes challenging. As such, these values may be able to motivate or even inspire you to act in ways that fit with what you hold to be important — rather than what is felt to be required (e.g. reaching the top of your chosen career, at any cost). This would involve clarifying what really is important for the individual and getting in touch with key principles that might guide them.

This of course, does not mean A/N individuals are people without any values. Rather, as a result of their driven personality, they often focus on goals. However, *goals are not the same as values* and learning the difference may open a window of opportunity for change. Goals are things we aim for, that can be achieved and then get ticked off from the lists that A/N individuals are so good at generating. There is no lack of ability within the A/N person to set and work towards goals. If anything, this skill set has become overdeveloped and, in the process of perfecting this, there has been some loss in terms of accounting for personal variables such as values. Values are a reflection and expression of the principles that are important to you as a person and will act as your guide through life if you connect with them.

However, you don't need to choose either goals *or* values. It is just that one of these tends to dominate things for A/N people. This sees people setting goals for a career 'pathway' and then resetting them (higher) once you have achieved the aim. There tends to be no problem for such folk in following a clear process to ensure that they are able to meet their goals in a timely and capable manner. Have you heard about setting SMART goals? This is great in terms of helping one learn to set goals for efficiency and to maximize the chances of achieving them. However, in my clinical experience, A/N people know this stuff and have been to numerous workshops on many variations of SMART goal-setting. Rather than go down that road again, it may be important to acknowledge that your goal-setting skills are at an acceptable level. Perhaps it is now time to balance this with other strategies and learn how to account for important factors such as personal values. For, in essence, it is the balancing aspect of the overall equation that is underdone for the A/N group. To help you obtain this balance, learn to reconnect with your values in order to account for other important aspects that are relevant to your unbalanced world. Those values might relate to family and personal relationships, and positive steps might include re-establishing friendships that have slipped away over time or re-exploring some cultural, artistic or recreational aspect that was once enjoyed or highly prized. Take time to think about what your values are.

AN EMPTY SPACE

A significant fear for the A/N person is around what might happen if they slow down with their mission or take time for themselves. Unfortunately, the automatic image generated from this notion of slowing down is often one of wasted time, empty space, self-indulgence and possibly not knowing what to do with the extra time. Remember, time and space have been successfully filled for a long time now by the intense focus on your chosen pursuit or career. The notion of not having something to work on can be, quite simply, scary. It is also unsettling, as most A/N individuals find it hard to generate options that they could do if they weren't so busy.

This is not the same as never having had any other dimensions to your personality, nor does it suggest that you have previously led a shallow and empty life. Rather, it is an indication of how much you have focused on particular issues, goals and tasks, often to the exclusion of things you once gained enjoyment and reinforcement from. It is perhaps now about reconfiguring your sense of self around what is valued and what might be good to revisit from the past.

It is no secret that high achievers in one domain usually have skills and abilities in other areas. Over time, though, the A/N person often shifts their attention, energy and focus from a range of activities to more specific and targetable issues — they become SMART about things. Such an approach makes sense in terms of rationalizing energy and resources so that effort can be concentrated for a better outcome from the 'important' task/s in life. However, it can prove to be a frustrating exercise for the A/N person to try to think what they might enjoy doing or to reflect upon what talents (other than their career-related ones) they possess. Interestingly, A/N people I have worked with often surprise themselves by recalling that they actually once enjoyed design or art or playing squash etc.

This 'new' approach to life is about helping you reorient your perspective, identify what you would like to do (but not *have* to do) and consider how you might prefer to spend your 'spare' time. This can be an important step towards starting to tap into what is meaningful for you as an individual, rather than useful as a team member. Consider for just an instant: if you had spare time, time that wasn't related to finishing a project or moving towards completion of a goal, how would you act? What would you do differently and why?

A relevant part of this process is looking at the positive changes that may come about, but also seeing this as an ongoing, active and sustainable aspect as you clarify how you want to engage with the world. Reconnecting with your values is not a destination or a chance to publicly say, 'I have certain values.' Rather, it is about identifying and relating to things that may well become signposts for your new journey in life. You may not have previously called them values. They may just have been things that inspired you towards a course of action or ways you acted because it felt 'right' or 'good'.

Of course, nothing in life is as simple as just deciding, 'I am going to change.' You can bet anything you like that, upon considering a change, your mind will immediately throw up reasons for not trying, why this won't work or how change may disrupt important and relevant issues already on the go. Such blocking is a result of the intense focus on tasks and ways of viewing life that have elevated goal attainment (and actions in pursuit of this) to the highest of levels. If you feel, however, that it is time to try to change, then get in touch with what is meaningful for you, rather than what is productive or efficient. If you get the hang of this 'strange' approach to life, you may start to notice a subtle change in some of the language that runs through your head. No longer will it all be about 'I have to', 'I should' or 'I must'. Now it may be about 'I would like to', 'That might be fun' or 'I wonder what might happen if …'. This perhaps is the beginning of a voyage of discovery or, more accurately, a renewed exploration, with different eyes and focus, of the worlds you already move within.

ACCEPTANCE EQUALS GIVING UP; OR DOES IT?

Alongside the ACT concept of flexibility sits the very useful and almost 'kind' approach of acceptance. This concerns a person's readiness to experience and thereby increase their capacity to tolerate things that feel uncomfortable. In particular, this approach highlights the internal appraisals and beliefs of the A/N person, which are often about the self and performance. As already mentioned, difficulties meeting goals are often interpreted as a failing, rather than a challenge to be overcome. Such people could benefit from learning to tolerate the associated unpleasant emotional experiences and the unhelpful memories that tend to come flooding in once a challenge is encountered.

If you struggle to accept this common human aspect of life (i.e. a less-than-perfect performance), then you may be at risk of heightened sensitivity to emotional difficulties. In particular, this could see anxiety and depression becoming a problem. However, the very issue of acceptance is a double-edged sword for the A/N person. It does not come naturally and discussing the concept of acceptance tends to bring up connotations of defeat. To 'accept' something means (for the A/N person) that it has beaten you, that you cannot find a solution and therefore it embodies images of rolling over and acknowledging that 'I have failed'. Rather than use the term acceptance, I tend to phrase the idea as 'accommodating' to the presence of unfamiliar emotions and/ or uncomfortable states and situations that cannot be 'fixed' but that that need to be worked alongside or managed.

Once the scene is set and language agreed upon, it is time to explore what 'accommodation' may actually mean for you, the A/N person. In essence, this is not an abandoning of control (a big fear for the A/N person). Rather, it embodies flexibility around being okay with some unsettling emotional states and not fearing them. If you can come to tolerate the presence of some worry and doubt, you might find it is possible to draw on a wider range of behaviours and responses that are not solely related to controlling the feelings. It will be helpful for you to learn that you can 'surf' your way through some levels of internal discomfort and, at other times, you can respond with strategies to manage the uncomfortable arousal that you are experiencing. This is accommodating to the presence of naturally occurring and understandable emotional responses to challenging situations. Although these feelings may be unsettling to the usually confident and dynamic A/N person, they are not in and of themselves pathological states. Indeed, a case could be made that ignoring or denying such experiences may actually lead along the road to pathology!

You do not need to be 'cured' of unhelpful thinking styles or emotional responses to disappointment. Such an expectation is an example of the A/N way of life (i.e. it is either present or it is gone, it is either helpful or evil etc.). Perhaps it is okay for these thoughts, beliefs and ways of viewing the world to be present? The issue isn't 'Did they pop up?' but rather 'Did I automatically respond to them in ways I did not fully appreciate or account for?' A better place to be is to allow these automatic thoughts and feelings to appear but be comfortable with the fact they can be fleeting responses, and then discriminate between the more or less helpful ones relevant to the circumstance and time. In essence, being able to be with these thoughts and feelings without slavishly implementing the automatic behaviours that often follow is an example of accommodation (or acceptance) and flexibility.

'I missed the deadline; I'm not up to it so I need to work much harder and faster' — in truth, this sort of statement holds little validity. The problem is that emotionally driven behaviour is seldom well thought through. A better option, perhaps, is to put the emphasis upon behaving in the most effective way in the current set of circumstances, with this particular set of contingencies. Notice how the emphasis here is shifting to the present, to what is happening *now*, and encouraging effective responding. Although this seems different to the stereotypical manner of responding for most A/N people, such an approach is actually speaking a language that can resonate with such individuals. It is about effectiveness and efficiency — key words that A/N people relate and aspire to.

WHAT'S IN A PERSPECTIVE?

You may be able to see from the above that we are talking about a personal perspective on internal events, and this notion can help us understand and, more importantly, address some of the traps the A/N person can fall into. Getting a handle on the 'me' that is involved in relating to our place in the world can help to bring about a new perspective, particularly related to the sense of who and what we are. This approach suggests that, over time, we come to relate to the person in the mirror as embodying and representing all the attributes that we have developed.

As a way of explaining this, McCracken and Velleman, in a 2010 article, describe the 'conceptualized self' as being an image we have of who we are, based on and built up from the attributes and stories of our life journey. The problem, as they point out, with this conceptualized self is that we can become strongly (and possibly non-discriminatingly) attached to its associated story. This can result in the aforementioned rigidity developing. In essence, there is a shorthand operating each time we see ourselves in the mirror and reflect upon who we are. This underscores the notion that: *this* is who I am, who I have always been and (unconsciously) who I will continue to be. The more that we connect with the ideals and descriptions we apply to ourselves, the more potential there is for these to define us. This can then roll over to directing what we do and how we go about things. If we think of and relate to ourselves as 'clever', 'hard working', (or alternatively) 'stupid' or 'incompetent', this can result in quite a restricted sense of self. One result of this is that we may become increasingly inflexible in how we see and relate to the world. This can happen with respect to our chosen roles in life as well. I could describe myself to a new acquaintance by saying, 'I am a clinical psychologist' or 'I am someone who does clinical psychology for a job.' Can you see any difference in the potential for one of those descriptions to be somewhat more restricting? So with respect to this conceptualized self, a challenge for A/N people can come when you strongly relate not only to the descriptor but all that it might mean or be thought to entail. Thus, once in a career, you may feel that to be truly successful you have to comply rigidly with the expectations and requests from others and also those obligations that you personally feel are attached to the position.

To help balance out the unhelpful aspects of over-identifying with the conceptualized self, it can be beneficial to explore what is involved with flexible perspective-taking. This allows a stepping back from the intimate involvement in a single view of life and encourages a perspective whereby the person sees themself as an observer of experiences. This is in contrast to being a bound-up participant who has no control over what seem like almost predetermined events and behaviours. This stepping-back hopefully encourages a new perspective-taking and aims to bring about comfort with and flexibility around the story of 'Who I am, was and will be'. It can assist us to see that we have built up an image (or is that a mirage?) around ourselves regarding what we do and how we need to act in the world. The problem with this self-image is that it is not fully fleshed out. Rather, it is more like a two-dimensional image printed on glass — one that can be seen clearly, that gives the impression of completeness but in reality has no flexibility or depth that can be worked with. As this imagery is experienced (and re-experienced) on such a regular basis (i.e. every time I reflect on who I am or go about doing something) it becomes a much encountered guidebook for life. As a result, we tend to go to the well-thumbed chapters in this guidebook that have previously helped us in unfamiliar places and eventually forget to question whether the information is as relevant now as it once was.

CASE STUDY

When I was doing my youthful travelling years ago, I came to rely upon a guidebook that most travellers had in their packs, from a series called *Let's Go*. This series presented information about countries and regions within their borders. It was trusted by travellers as being a guide to the best sights, yummiest (and cheapest) food and the local attractions. It helped guide my plans and the things I considered spending my rapidly vanishing funds upon.

However, I eventually came to understand that the information was obtained by students travelling the previous year (or earlier) and that, with the best will possible, this information could not be seen as 'current' nor was it possible to update it in any quick manner. As I had already invested money in this weighty tome I continued to use it as my direction finder (yes, dear reader, this was before the time of smartphones and iPad apps), even in the face of information and experiences that indicated it was not current or always that useful. Time had simply moved on but I and many others were still trying to apply the information from what had been (generally) a useful and trustworthy source. This meant that sometimes travellers anticipated things that were not deliverable or encountered situations that were different to what they were expecting.

I recall a scene at the Library of Celsus, at Ephesus in Turkey, surely one of the most amazing sites remaining from antiquity. On this occasion, two young English-speaking women were remonstrating with the official at the site on admission costs. It was their contention that they should be charged a particular price based on the amount quoted in their guidebook. The hapless official patiently pointed to the sign which clearly indicated the current admission prices while the tenacious young women waved their copy of *Let's Go* and attempted to get the official to not only read the 'proof' but adjust his charges accordingly. Eventually, it became clear that the official was not going to budge and the travellers were faced with a choice: either pay what was advertised or miss out on entrance. These two young women took what they considered to be the moral high ground, refused to pay what was asked and left.

Rather than the above case study exemplifying a matter of principle, I would suggest it is a beautiful example of rigidly adhering to guidelines that are held to be true and then not adjusting or demonstrating any flexibility — despite clear indications that the approach is no longer valid or useful. In this case, holding onto the outdated guidelines came at a cost in terms of what these travellers encountered on their trip. If you have never seen this amazing building with all its memories and indicators of a past and glorious life, Google the 'Library of Celsus' and see just what these young people missed out on. I wonder how their day and their experiences may have been different if they had not relied on previously recorded information and their belief in this? How might their lives and memories have been enriched if they could have shifted a bit, been more flexible with their expectations and decision-making processes?

Similar to this, if we become too attached to who we are or have been — and therefore to what we feel we 'should' do — there is a risk of repeating the same actions and responses even if they are proving to be less than useful. For the A/N person the risk is in tightly holding onto ways of behaving because this is 'who I am' . . . or, rather, who I believe myself to be. By learning to step back a little from the descriptors of ourselves and the image we relate to, we will still be able to maintain a sense of 'who I am' but have greater flexibility.

A BETTER VIEW BY STEPPING BACK

Perhaps the issue relevant to A/N individuals is that that their view of themselves may lack balance and perspective. This, of course, makes it hard to see things from any other angle or consider if decisions could have been taken differently and therefore led to another outcome. To do this requires some ability to distance ourselves psychologically from the story in our head. There can be some real positives from being able to de-automate this way of seeing ourselves and our relationship to our workplace or chosen pursuit. What if we could develop an awareness that we are part of something yet are also able to watch and consider what is going on at the time?

It is this issue of perspective that may be useful for the A/N individual. Of value is identifying that we have thoughts but they are not necessarily the totality of 'me' nor are they a call to action that cannot be ignored. Rather, coming to realize that we can have thoughts and feelings (e.g. 'I must work hard all the time', 'Every task needs to be perfect') but also observe them from a psychological distance without being slavishly directed by them may potentially become liberating. This freedom comes from not being completely attached to these thoughts and feelings or having an investment in these being enacted in a particular way, timeframe or with a certain outcome. As a result, 'good enough' may start to be an okay thing! By observing a thought and not automatically following it, we can start to prise apart this sense that 'I am what I think, which is me'. As a result, your sense of who you are can remain intact and healthy as it is not bound up in the content of the thought. The thoughts, the ideas or the plans are just that: thoughts, ideas and plans. Radical, huh?

Unfortunately for the A/N person, there has often been a longstanding blurring of the boundaries between the self and the thinking. This can result in a drive to complete the ideas and plans, as they are experienced as being intimately associated with 'me' and 'who I am' — with associated risks for identity and mood. There is a melding of the person and the thoughts which get expressed via (internally) demanding phrases such as 'I must always . . .'. Note the lack of wriggle room with this internal language and the fact the individual has meshed with the thought. This is where the idea of stepping back (figuratively speaking) from the thinking process may well be of assistance. The approach can be conceived of as a way of monitoring or watching thoughts and processes as they come along, without being caught up with them and any associated feelings that are attached to these thoughts (e.g. 'I can't leave the office until everything is finished.'). The aim is to learn how to observe thoughts and ideas like someone who is simply there to document what happens but not to intervene or promote any behaviour (a bit like a naturalist in Africa observing a pride of lions). By adopting this approach, it is hoped that you can make and maintain the distinction between yourself and the thoughts and internal drivers (e.g. to do a perfect job or to prove you are the most reliable person in the company) you experience.

The important thing to realize is that the content of the idea is quite separate to who and what the person is. Just as a firefighter is not his or her uniform, you are not your thoughts. The professional firefighter retains knowledge about fires and safety issues at all times but s/he is not always part of the team required to put out fires. They have time out from that role and its demands and do not have to respond to the siren on their days off. A helpful approach would be for you to be able to move into the observer or one-step-removed role as and when needed — that is, to not feel obligated to always respond to or follow through on the demanding thoughts you have. This does not mean total detachment from every aspect of your life, but rather having the ability to identify and distinguish when unhelpful or pressurizing thoughts are present and then to know how to slip into the observing role. This can bring about an enhanced sense of control, one that is appropriate to the situation in front of you — rather than vainly trying to be totally in control of all things at all times. In such a case, you can choose whether to follow the thoughts or an alternative path which may make other options available.

Why such an approach is important is that the A/N person tends to become trapped by cognitive processes that are built around the powerful rules and approaches learnt early in life. To be fair, though, most people operate by general rules to some extent and these impact on their decisions. During recent renovations, a friend's son entered the kitchen asking for a drink of water. However, the tap was out of action so it was suggested he go to the bathroom and get a drink from the tap there. The son's immediate response (accompanied by one of those priceless teenaged facial expressions that clearly intimate Dad is insane) was 'Don't be so gross' and 'That's beyond wrong!'. My friend pointed out that his son used that tap and water to clean his teeth twice daily plus that the water for both areas came from the same source; but it made no difference. One was where drinking water came from and the other was apparently 'cleaning'-type water! Now, the son is a smart young man and not irretrievably trapped by age or convention but I guess he had been socialized into seeing that you normally drink water and clean your teeth in different places, and never the twain shall meet!

So while we may be dealing with a usual process here, A/N people seem to have developed this into a bit of an art form, and therefore it may have greater implications for how you engage in activity. With these cognitive processes directing things, there is a risk of becoming rigid in applying the 'rules' around how things should be done. If you are unable to be flexible at times of challenge and difficulty, you might retreat into your well-rehearsed coping behaviours. Invariably, this means pushing yourself harder, longer and more consistently, even in the face of evidence that this is no longer bearing fruit. It is suggested that you might benefit from being able to disengage from these rules, cognitions and belief systems as and when needed. One of the aims of changing this A/N style of responding is to provide a flexible approach to situations and try to ensure responses are not unduly restricted or narrowed by the internal language, beliefs and thoughts.

IN SUMMARY

One of the best ways to respond to a changing environment is to be able to choose from options. This requires the ability to shift between these options and be open to choosing the one that best suits the current situation. One of the challenges for the A/N personality is that you tend to work within a narrowed perspective and may see limited options (e.g. work harder or make it perfect). Doing things on autopilot seems easier and more familiar but it may not allow you to account for variations or new demands within the work environment.

The Harsh Internal Critic is often viewed as a mechanism to keep ourselves on track and 'in with a chance'. However, we have now seen that this voice contains many (oft repeated) negative messages that can undermine our sense of self. The difficulty is that we give this voice too much credence and we find ourselves wrapped up in the thoughts and responding to the 'rules' that we consider go along with these messages. The result is that we narrow our perspective and retreat to a place where responses are easily generated and understood (i.e. 'Don't stop for any reason.'). But . . . what if this voice could be shaped or altered into a motivational or supportive voice, one with helpful advice?

Acceptance is not a dirty word, despite what your A/N learning leads you to believe. It is not about giving in. It is about being open to options and experiences, not just fighting and trying to defeat something; about working alongside and managing the situation, not running from it or trying to dominate it. You don't have to give up your control — in fact, you might find yourself feeling more in control if you account for the realities of a situation and acknowledge the feelings you are experiencing. This will allow you to see what is happening for you *here and now* and may help you to find the best approach for managing the current situation, rather than simply doing what has always been expected. A move from recycling old ways through to considering newer options is a big step forward but one that will come about more readily if you drop the attack mode and accommodate the reality of the situation.

Developing a new perspective on your current challenge or wider life can help you to generate new, different or simply more options for responding. If you can step back from the intense involvement with the situation, you will be able to observe more clearly what is happening or what is about to happen. It is perhaps time to consider letting go of the guidelines you have relied on for so long and trust that you may be able to make your way forward without that well-worn roadmap of your life. Realize that you are infinitely more than the outline or description of what you have done before. Sure, acknowledge when and how these 'rules' and approaches have helped. But also see what can be generated from this idea of stepping back and considering things. You may just surprise yourself in terms of your creativity and novel problem-solving attributes. You are you and not just what you have previously done. Similarly, you are not the thoughts that you have, nor do they represent fully who you are or everything you are capable of!

ASPECTS FOR REFLECTION, OPTIONS FOR CHANGE

To begin the shift towards flexibility in your life, you might like to embark on a positive process of reconfiguring your sense of self. This is not giving up on who you have been and it is especially not seeking a completely new persona. Rather, it is about getting in touch with your own values and letting them guide you with your choices and actions. If these things are aligned, you are more likely to be heading in a direction that will not only be satisfying but also more sustainable. The beauty of this approach is that you don't need to find someone new to become; you will notice that the attributes and building blocks are already present and have been for a long time. The problem is that they have become out of balance and some important aspects of yourself may have slipped to the background. Perhaps it is time to find out (or is that rediscover?) what these important aspects are. Reconfiguring is not the same as rebuilding; it is more about shuffling the positive traits and abilities that have always been present. These may have, up to now, been ordered and prioritized to bring about the achievements and high-level outcomes within your A/N lifestyle.

However, much like a deck of cards, a bit of timely shuffling can often result in a much more useful hand to play within the next game . . . or chapter in your life.

So what is important to you and how might you like your life to be lived from here on in? Why not take some time to consider what it is that is truly important to you. This is about who and what you really want to be like, not what you think you *should* be like. If you can get in touch with these things that many people call 'values', they may help adjust those powerful schemas that have been driving you through life to this point. It is more about tapping into a purpose for your life rather than resetting a goal. I would suggest that you don't need to learn anything about the latter — you already have that part down pat! Let's try and see if you can identify what you really want from, and within, key domains in your life.

Try this

Set out on the next page are some key areas of life. Choose one or more that is relevant to you and your A/N existence to this point. Under your chosen heading/s, list the values you would like to demonstrate daily and live by — a couple of examples are provided to start you off. Remember, values are about the personal qualities you would like to exhibit in each domain (rather than goals such as to be rich or to be the boos) but perhaps haven't been able to due to the specific focus on outcomes that is part of your A/N lifestyle.

Work	To be proud of my performance but not let this dominate my life
Physical activity	
Family	To be available for my kids and share time in the evenings
Arts/hobbies	

Once you have completed this, try to consider what your life might be like when you live according to these important aspects. This may lead you on to considering what you might need to change in your life to begin balancing things out.

. . . .

Another question to explore at this point is whether it might be okay to consider looking at things from a different perspective. Is it okay to be a bit kinder with and to yourself when you encounter a challenging situation? Rather than pushing on with over-familiar approaches to life that don't permit flexibility, maybe it is time to pull back and re-identify those things that are actually important for you — rather than those you feel are important to do. Shifting away from the focus on setting goals may permit you to develop a better balance between those should-dos and want-to-dos. When was the last time you actually accounted for the personally important things rather than responding with the externally demanded or expected behaviours? This is not about becoming self-indulgent (for that is the fear of the A/N person). Rather, it is about finding some degree of middle ground. No, this is not shirking or giving up; this is standing back, looking at all the options and considering what *you choose* to do here, in this situation, at this time.

Try this

This is a strategy for those who are particularly keen, to help you begin the process of learning to view things from another perspective. If you can get the feel of how to do this, you may be able to shift to another, more helpful view on any given situation and then see if it brings up any options for responding that you had not previously considered. It may also permit you to see that you don't have to beat up on yourself because things were not 'perfect'.

Let's try some visualization. All you will need for this exercise is a pen, some paper and your imagination. Imagine that you are an interviewer for a television science show. You are presenting a show on colour blindness and you are going to interview a person who lives with this condition. Your task is to get across to the audience just what it is like to live with colour blindness, how it impacts a person's life, and to give a feel for what it might be like to experience this. Prior to starting the visualization, take a few minutes to think about what questions you'd like to ask the 'interviewee' and write them down on a sheet of paper. Remember, you are trying to help people gain an understanding of life from the interviewee's point of view. Therefore, try to use open, 'wondering' questions that will help you and others understand something you have not personally experienced and may not have ever considered. Think about how the viewers need to hear this information so that they can make sense of and work with this new knowledge.

Now that you have your questions, settle back in a comfortable, quiet place with no distractions. Relax yourself into the chair, close your eyes and see yourself on the set of a television program. Visualize all the detail of the surroundings, as if you are really in that room. Once you can see the scene and also your interviewee, engage him/her in conversation and lead into the questions you have prepared. This is where the perspective-taking aspect comes in — allow this person to answer your questions in as much detail as they want. Yes, it is you 'putting words in their mouth' and that is the whole point of the exercise. If 'they' can answer the questions in a way that represents life with colour blindness, you are actually shifting from your perspective to that of another.

Practise this a few times and then try using this new ability of considering another perspective the next time you encounter a challenging situation. This may allow you to step aside from your usual response set and consider something new or different in terms of how you see the problem or situation, what you can do about it and then how you talk to yourself about it.

. . . .

This chapter is not trying to suggest that it is easy to adapt, to accommodate and to become more flexible. It takes time to develop the necessary skills and they cannot always be put into place immediately to alter the direction of events or responses. To reinforce this point, I offer the following observation. My wife and I were returning from several weeks travelling through countries that promoted a very casual standard of dress. On the final leg of the flight home, we entered the plane's cabin only to be directed to palatial-looking seats in business class. The elusive and oft dreamed about upgrade had finally happened. However, we were clothed like dishevelled bohemians and looking as if we would be more at home in a beach hut. Talk about negative cognitions and strong emotions racing in; uncomfortable doesn't even begin to cover this! No matter how I tried, I found it difficult to settle back into the luxurious environment and enjoy the gratis goodies. I also recall struggling to figure out how to use the entertainment system but could not bring myself to ask for assistance as this would surely prove to the staff that I did not usually fly business class. So, there I was, sitting in luxury and completely unable to enjoy the experience as my head was full of negative talk and my gut was consumed with angst around being identified as a fraud. Darwin would be horrified at my inability to size up the environment, modify my actions and fit in!

9 The partner's journey

Throughout the book I have been concentrating on ways of identifying and understanding what happens to, for and within the A/N individual. However, alongside these individuals there often are travel-weary partners who have been there for a journey that they didn't perhaps always comprehend. These good folk have seen repeating patterns of behaviour and realized these were potentially problematic but perhaps did not know what they could do to help or bring about some change.

There is usually a rather special dance that develops between the A/N person and their partner. Here we are talking about the woman or man who has waited patiently at home as the time of the concert draws ever near, or watched as the dinner they cooked spoils in the oven due to the partner not arriving home as expected. These people tend to have shown exceptional tolerance and patience as they (repeatedly) hear the promises to the kids about an upcoming outing while knowing full well that something else may take precedence.

Many of these partners have known in their heart of hearts that the extent of the behaviours they have witnessed and tolerated is not 'usual'. Often they have wondered why their special person has to be so dedicated and focused upon achieving goal after goal after goal. The partner has essentially been engaged in this journey at multiple levels. On the one hand they have been an observer, one who has been a step removed from the behaviour but nonetheless able to view what is happening . . . and may well continue to happen. The partner is often conflicted within this role. For the most part, they want to support their special person with each endeavour and hope that they reach their goals and dreams. However, they also spend a fair chunk of their time filling in the gaps and explaining to children, family and friends why the whole family can't make it to a particular occasion.

CASE STUDY

Rebecca is a capable professional who has come to understand that her husband embodies many characteristics of the A/N personality-style. He has been involved with his own business for a number of years and this has been taking ever-increasing amounts of his time and energy. Recently, the importance of this venture has become a focal point for the A/N characteristics that we have been reading about. This has resulted in Rebecca's husband spending increasing amounts of time on work-related issues as well as being at the workplace for longer hours, and Rebecca has found that there is less time for them as a couple. She has also noticed that her husband's stress levels have been much higher and that he finds it hard to wind down from the demands of the expanding enterprise. Additionally, he is increasingly experienced as 'grumpy', more often tired and less attentive, plus he is experiencing increasingly disturbed sleep patterns. Another aspect of note is that the work plans and issues tend to dominate all conversations between the couple.

Despite Rebecca being a tactful and caring person, she is struggling to help her husband see the negative impact upon him of working so intensely over such a long period. She is also starting to find herself alone in a relationship, which she can now articulate is not really what she signed up for in the marriage.

It is not uncommon to hear stories similar to Rebecca's when you work with people who live alongside someone with the A/N personality-style. Over the years, I have seen some strong similarities between the family lives of A/N people — a case of different faces but the same story. Although most of the partners I have worked with have been women, this is by no means an absolute or a given. There are numerous women who exhibit A/N behaviours and their partners have stories to tell that are similar to what is being outlined in this section. As I have tried to previously identify, A/N characteristics and behaviours are not exclusive to a particular gender, and therefore the partner who may be affected can be of either gender, whether this be in a heterosexual or same-sex relationship. S/he is invariably supportive and encouraging but often finds this to become somewhat of a trap — one where they feel they must continue to offer support, despite seeing unhelpful and sometimes unpleasant changes within their partner.

Life alongside an A/N individual can become frustrating and somewhat lonely as s/he focuses increasing amounts of their energy upon the project at hand or future aspects of this. The demands of the task can see the person working longer hours, often outside of their previous usual pattern, which can bring about alterations to family life and expectations. Partners describe that they need to fit in with the increasing demands of the workplace or organization and that this can lead to a loss of personal identity and their own goal achievement. The latter may also be around what can be done as a couple or a family after the usual working-week hours or on weekends. It becomes hard to plan for outings and events, which can lead to the realization that it is often easier to arrange things for and by oneself. Over time, this becomes an easier option and then a familiar one *but* at no time have I heard a partner say that this was their preferred option.

A challenging time (or crisis point) can arise in the relationship when the non-A/N partner encounters some difficulties of their own. I have noticed that in such situations, a number of partners feel they should not 'trouble' the A/N person, who is often perceived as being busy, focused and under pressure. This leaves the partner holding back and not expressing or addressing their own issues and needs. Often the partner's personal needs are, unfortunately, viewed as something the already busy and stressed A/N person does not need added to their plate. As a result, the partner can be left to continue dealing with the day-to-day issues and also make their own way through the emotional or physical challenges confronting them. At one level, this seems to be viewed as how it has become, while at another level I have had partners describe the situation as 'frustrating', 'unfair' and as though such a situation is devaluing who they are.

ASPECTS FOR THE A/N PERSON TO CONSIDER

All the above can take its toll on the partner. So . . . why haven't you, the A/N individual, noticed? This is the person you are sharing your life with and see each day. I guess it may be hard to realize that there have been things happening that you have not really taken on board. Most of the A/N people I have worked with continue to have a deep sense of love and caring for their partners. It comes as a shock to the A/N individual to hear that their partner might feel as if they have grown apart to some degree. I have noticed that this is not necessarily due to a change in feelings but rather because less time is shared and communication is happening at a reduced or changed level. The A/N person seems to be genuinely shocked to realize that there are new systems and ways of doing things around the home. That these new patterns have developed out of necessity — to fill the gap that came about due to their increasingly lengthy absence — seems also to be quite a surprise.

So what's it like for your partner? Partners often describe a sense of being somewhat trapped. They tend to be proud that their special person (you) is succeeding but also saddened that there is a third party in the relationship — the career or special project. This is a rival that is hard to compete with, given the positives around potential success and advancement. Such an intruder is also complex and intangible, with an unexplained but powerful grasp on the A/N individual. The sadness experienced by the partner doesn't seem to be coming from a place of jealousy. Rather, it is about seeing how their special person is striving so hard and perhaps, over time, enjoying the challenge less and less while seemingly being unable to break away from whatever the task or goal is. It is also about noticing a subtle change within their person over time, such that priorities no longer represent mutual goals and desires. It can be about altering family scheduling to help avoid the clash between family routines and business meetings after working hours.

It can be hard for a partner to try to tell you, the A/N person, that they are worried about you only to hear that everything is 'okay' and under control. It can be frustrating to plan things and then have to cancel them due to a clash with work commitments. It can be upsetting to see the kids yet again not able to have Mum or Dad come along to the school production.

It can be bewildering to realize the A/N partner cannot see what is so blindingly obvious: that they are working harder and starting to get run down. It can also be heartbreaking to see the one they love start to doubt themselves and become less confident in areas they previously excelled in and were passionate about.

CASE STUDY

Sara was trying to make sense of what had gone wrong in her relationship and where it might be headed. She described being married to a man who was very talented within the IT field. He had apparently been employed by a company that became highly successful on the back of his knowledge, skills and work ethic. However, it took its toll and this man became depressed and extremely anxious, to the point he could not cope with day-to-day tasks, let alone work-based ones.

Sara stepped up and looked after all aspects of family life while her husband recovered over a period of months. She described that this was a very tiring and emotionally draining time, as she also needed to find employment to help with the finances. Interestingly, Sara did not describe this as the greatest challenge to their relationship. What was most confusing for Sara was that once her husband's depression lifted, he immediately formulated plans to start up his own IT company. This saw him operating from home, with no boundaries around the hours he put in; he began rising before 6 a.m. to start the day's productivity and worked through till late at night. By all accounts, he worked and lived alongside the family but was so focused on setting up his own company that he had minimal interaction with them. Despite much discussing, arguing and pleading, nothing Sara said could alter her husband's behaviour. As far as he was concerned the 'problem' (i.e. the depression) was long gone. Now it was business as usual, with potential for greater, self-directed success.

A case of symptoms being addressed but the cause of the problem being ignored, perhaps?

ASPECTS FOR THE PARTNER TO CONSIDER

Life is not a one-way street. In fact, it is more of a tango that we dance with our partners: a complex rhythm that has well rehearsed patterns to it, and the more familiar these steps are, the easier the movement and flow becomes. If you have identified with some of the descriptions above, then perhaps there is a lot going on in your family and relationship. However, as noted earlier, this book isn't about apportioning blame but, rather, trying to bring about understanding and clarity that may facilitate movement towards a better state of affairs.

For you, the partner, there may also be some aspects of how you engage and interact that may open up opportunities for helping to bring about this change. So far, we have noted how you might have adapted (out of necessity) to maintain the family and its progress. However, this positive adaptation may have also allowed situations to develop that reinforce certain patterns, which in turn make it more likely the behaviours of concern will continue e.g. the scheduling of meetings 'after hours'. If your deft and subtle balancing acts maintain harmony and peace in the family's world, potential problems may be unrecognized by the A/N person. If you view these changes as being unavoidable or you identify with the pressures upon the person, then you will be more likely to act in ways that help those behaviours to remain in place. This may have initially been for very sound reasons, of course (e.g. you are very caring, you are aware of the potential costs to the family unit or perhaps you even share some of the A/N traits and therefore over-identify with what the person is going through). I am suggesting that the social/familial context these behaviours occur in can have a bearing upon how well they are tolerated or reinforced.

The key questions now are around whether things need to remain this way. There is often little point in simply going on about how and why things got to this particular juncture — that's what this book is doing for you (i.e. helping people make sense of the A/N personality-style). Rather, it may now be about what do *we*, the two partners, want to do about this and where do you see things heading. Worrying about how one ended up at a particular destination is not helpful at the very moment you are trying to decide whether this is an okay place to stay or one to move on from. The soul searching can come a little bit later, perhaps. This is not to say that it is not important; indeed, this very book you are reading is predicated on the fact that it is vital to gain an understanding and develop some insight into the effects of a life characterized by the A/N approach. However, now may be the time to reconnect and affirm a mutual (between you and the A/N person) understanding that things are not as they were and are not as they were intended to be. Ask yourself: is it okay to move towards some change, and might there be some benefits from this for the A/N individual, you (the partner) and your family? If the answer is yes, then exploring all the variables and behaviours within this book may help you both to see where things went off track and why they have stayed that way for some time. An enhanced understanding may also be one of the keys to opening up the potential for a different future — that is, a future based on positive change that encompasses a better understanding of issues, as well as permitting change without completely overhauling either the relationship or the individual.

IN SUMMARY

This way of life takes two to Tango. The A/N person often needs someone helping to deal with life's daily challenges in order to free them up to focus on the task(s) at hand. The partner is involved by way of filling in the gaps and managing the myriad challenges that come up from the A/N person not being around. Both people in this dance may be doing things to an extreme such that an unhelpful system is maintained — to the possible detriment of all involved.

The A/N person may be distracted from 'real life' due to their focused nature. However, what they often see around them is a household that runs well and things that (magically) get sorted. This means that the partner's excellent coping is what is on display and this can lead to a false sense of everything running well i.e. there is no problem. If the partner does not share just how much effort is required to maintain this equilibrium it might not be noticed and therefore, awareness/understanding may have no chance to develop.

Partners have a limit to their tolerance but this isn't necessarily signalled as having been reached — until it is too late. They can end up feeling distant, shut-out and less connected. They may also find a path of least resistance and establish routines and ways of doing things that don't include the A/N person!

Behaviours that seem so necessary within the work situation or your personal philosophy may be trapping the A/N individual into ways of acting. If you haven't acknowledged this or explored it for yourself, it may be difficult to see what it is doing to significant others i.e. your partner and family.

Maybe now is a good time to see if both of you wish to continue with this dance or perhaps consider whether it is time to change and explore how things might be different for all involved.

ASPECTS FOR REFLECTION, OPTIONS FOR CHANGE

The suggestions below are broken up into sections for you (the A/N person), your partner and both of you as a couple.

If you are an A/N person reading this book

Your partner is important! S/he is also the one most directly affected by your behaviours.

Use the information in this book to reflect on how things may have got off track with your family life. Be open to and consider the possibility that there is another (valid) perspective to how things are operating in your life: your partner's. Try to consider what it has been like for her/him living alongside you as you have focused most of your energy and efforts on the tasks and roles you considered to be important. If you can see that there may have been some challenges for your partner, perhaps it is time to talk this through together.

If you have been so busy that you have had no time and energy for the 'usual' family things, you might be feeling abandoned by the family as they get on with their lives. You may be feeling overwhelmed or worn out by all the effort you have expended over a long period of time. However, if you cannot clearly express your feelings and accurately describe what you need from your partner, it is hard for them to support you.

Listen to and be genuinely interested in your partner's point of view. Let them express things in their way, not in words you prefer to hear. Acknowledge and validate the feelings and challenges your partner is telling you about.

What if the fear of being judged has become so strong that you can't let your partner know you are actually feeling trapped or are struggling? However, if you don't try to share what is happening you might miss the opportunity to gain some support with the challenges you are facing.

If you are the partner reading this book

Central to making and sustaining change will be for the A/N person to develop an appreciation of how their behaviours affect you, along with an understanding of where this approach to life may have come from. If you are the one who has purchased this book, get your busy partner to start reading (*there is no time like the present!*). Maybe choose a key chapter and get them to read that before encouraging that the whole book be digested.

Your A/N partner needs to gain some insight into themselves before they can try to change. Remember, their personality-style has been directing their behaviour for many years. Time to reflect will also be important and necessary — don't place unfair burdens on them to have read a few pages and then have an 'aha' moment. This whole thing might be 'news' to them and, as such, they might have no idea how to begin the change process or even know that this is required.

Be open to considering that some of your behaviours could be maintaining aspects of the situation. If your caring nature is such that you prioritize the needs of your partner and feel the need to fix up problems (and potential problems), there might be no need for the A/N person to change. Why would s/he when everything seems to get sorted out?

Although this has been a hard journey for you, resist the temptation to demand change and make it happen *now*. It will take time to understand what has been going on and change will be something that needs to be tried on for size. There will undoubtedly be both gains and some slippage with respect to bringing about a change to how one interacts with the world. Don't become despondent if things are not brand new after the first trial at modifying behaviour!

If you are reading this book as a couple

If you can both gain an appreciation of how life has altered, you may be able to work collaboratively to bring about changes that are beneficial for the whole family. Being honest about how you both feel is important, but remember: how you share this honesty is also important. Change is a process. As such, giving feedback and being open (both parties) to hearing this will enhance the effectiveness of the changes you are trying to implement. You are bound to get better and more durable outcomes if the strategies you choose to implement are agreed upon and seem relevant to both of you.

As has been said in many books and therapeutic situations, communication is the key. Given that the people reading this book may be pressed for time, the focus perhaps should be on the quality of your interactions. You might even need to book a time together in the early stages — this is not colluding with the business approach but simply being practical. If there is a mismatch between what you say and what you want to say, opportunities will be lost. It won't be enough to listen to what is being said; you will need to hear it. Remember, even if you have been together for many years, you really cannot read the other person's mind so don't expect them to do the same for you and know what you really want. Believing that your partner 'should' understand your needs and where you are coming from is not really fair.

Getting the best out of your efforts to communicate will come from openly sharing how you feel. Of course, how each partner responds is also central to making positive gains. If you can both show some empathy and demonstrate that you have listened to and actually heard what is being said, the channels of communication are more likely to remain open and changes to behaviour sustained. What's that saying about listening with more than your ears?

. . . .

Following are two tasks you might like to try with your partner. Please note that these are optional.

Try this

Together, come up with six specific challenges or concerns that the A/N approach to life may be presenting for the two of you and (if relevant) your family.

1. _____
_____

2. _____
_____

3. _____
_____

4. _____
_____

5. _____
_____

6. _____
_____

Now, write down — together — three key behaviours or issues from the above that you would like to see change.

1. _____
   _____

2. _____
   _____

3. _____
   _____

Try this

Try to take the perspective of *the other person* and write down three thoughts about or responses to the questions below.

1. For the A/N person: What might it be like to be the partner of someone who is so focused on work, sport or artistic pursuits?

1. _____
   _____

2. _____
   _____

3. _____
   _____

2. For the partner: What might it be like to feel that you must always put everything into the task in front of you, despite the costs to yourself?

1. _____

_____

2. _____

_____

3. _____

_____

References

Agassi, A. 2009, *Open: An autobiography*, Three Rivers Press, New York.

Bamber, M. & McMahon, R. 2008, 'Danger — early maladaptive schemas at work! The role of early maladaptive schemas in career choice and the development of occupational stress in health workers', *Clinical Psychology and Psychotherapy*, 15, pp. 96–112.

Ellam-Dyson, V. & Palmer, S. 2010, 'Rational coaching with perfectionistic leaders to overcome avoidance of leadership responsibilities', *The Coaching Psychologist*, vol. 6, no. 2, pp. 81–7.

Hayes, S.C., Luoma, J.B., Bond, F.W., Masuda, A. & Lillis, J. 2006, 'Acceptance and Commitment Therapy: Model, processes and outcomes', *Behaviour Research and Therapy*, 44, pp. 1–25.

Hopkins, V. & Gardner, D. 2012, 'The mediating role of work engagement and burnout in the relationship between job characteristics and psychological distress among lawyers', *New Zealand Journal of Psychology*, vol. 41, no. 1, pp. 59–68.

Lunenburg, F.C. 2011, 'Self-efficacy in the workplace: Implications for motivation and performance', *International Journal of Management, Business and Administration*, vol. 14, no. 1.

Mahoney, A.E & McEvoy, P.M. 2011, 'A transdiagnostic examination of intolerance of uncertainty across anxiety and depressive disorders', *Cognitive Behaviour Therapy*, pp. 1–11.

McCracken, L.M. & Velleman, S.C. 2010, 'Psychological flexibility in adults with chronic pain: A study of acceptance, mindfulness and values-based action in primary care', *Pain*, 148, pp. 141–7.

van Beek, I., Hu, Q., Schaufeli, W.B., Taris, T.W. & Schreurs, B.H.J. 2012, 'For fun, love, or money: What drives workaholic, engaged and burned-out employees at work?', *Applied Psychology: An International Review*, 61 (1), pp. 30–55.

Index